D0842294

Man with a Racket

Man with a Racket

The Autobiography of
Pancho Gonzales

as told to
CY RICE

A. S. Barnes and Company · New York

79167

© 1959 by A. S. Barnes and Company, Inc.

Library of Congress Catalog Card Number: 59-7068

Printed in the United States of America
by The Colonial Press Inc., Clinton, Mass.

To my friends of the Olympic Tennis Club,
Exposition Park, Los Angeles.

Preface

When my agent, Alex Jackinson, first suggested that I sign Pancho Gonzales to a contract and help him construct his life story, I jumped at the chance. Six months later I still wanted to jump—but this time straight at Mr. Jackinson, landing feet first on tender parts of his anatomy.

"What a fine opportunity," wrote Mr. Jackinson. "Here's the greatest tennis player in the world and no book on him. Get it!"

Being a novice at biographical writing, I asked for instructions. They were delightfully simple. "Just sit down in a big easy chair with a notebook," counseled Mr. Jackinson. "Then he tells his life story, you listen, you make notes, and it all comes out in the proper sequence."

This sounded fine in theory. Only it wasn't workable. Sure, I could sit down without suffering any hardship. I sit down all day anyway. The trouble was that Pancho wouldn't sit. Pancho can't sit. Sitting, no matter how you look at it, isn't vio-

lent exercise, which eliminates any expected cooperation
from Mr. Gonzales.

Pancho is perpetual motion. Something seems to be chasing him and he seems to be chasing something. Whatever it
is, I wish he'd catch up with it; or it would catch up with him.
If I'd known then what I do now, and had been given a choice
of helping put the book together or climbing Mt. Everest,
barefooted and in my shorts, I would have taken the latter.

Our initial talk lasted one hour. Between pleadings, cajol-
ings, and mild threats, Pancho intermittently grunted a few
monosyllables, all extremely pertinent to the conflict in the
story. They were either "yes" or "no." At the end of the hour
he arose and said, "Well, there's my life story. Just put it together."

I'd have enjoyed taking Pancho apart and putting him together again. However, this time by jigsawing the human
figure I'd create him so that he'd have two posteriors—one
in the conventional place and one in the front. Then he'd
have to sit oftener and longer.

Interviewing Pancho is analogous to squeezing a slippery tube of tooth paste with a blocked passage. Nothing, of
course, comes out. The feasible approach is to hurl him to the
floor, tie him up with chains. I'm not strong enough to accomplish this. Few persons are.

So how do you pin down a whirling dervish? The answer
is: You don't. You just follow the dervish and go into a spin
with it. The drawback is that I never came out of it. I've
hurled questions at him while he was taking a shower, board-
ing a plane, between serves on the court—just about everywhere but underwater. I've hounded his very footsteps, got
into his hair at every possible opportunity.

I don't think he likes me very much.

I have no real proof of this except from a remark he made
to me that "I never started locking doors around my house

until I met you." Maybe he said this because I followed him into the bathroom, about the only place where I had him all to myself.

There was the day I blew my top. Four weeks had frittered by. I had three scribbled pages of notes.

"Pancho," I said over the telephone, "I want one full day with you."

"Any time," he said obligingly.

"Tomorrow," I suggested.

"Tomorrow," he agreed.

I said, "I'll be over early."

"Come any time," he said.

Simple as that.

I reached the Gonzales' house at 9:00 A.M. Pancho, together with his wife, Henrietta, and three young sons, was having breakfast. Breakfast, throughout the world, is recognized as a quiet meal where people drink coffee slowly and begin conditioning their reflexes for the day.

No such custom prevailed at the Gonzales' house. Pandemonium reigned. The telephone rang incessantly, the children argued, boxer pups kept leaping at me, and the friskiest tried teething on my ankle bone. One of them ran off with my notebook. Breakfast over, Pancho headed for the Los Angeles Tennis Club and I climbed into his car with him. This was going to be wonderful. At long last I had him trapped, sitting three inches away from me with no possible outside interference.

I started a question. It never reached the vocal stage. It stuck in my throat, disappeared from my mind. All I kept thinking was: "I'm too young to die." Pancho was turning traffic-laden Wilshire into another Indianapolis Speedway. I shut my eyes; I clutched the door; I think I prayed a little.

At the tennis club his entrance signaled a flying welter of human bodies—strapping muscular bodies—eagerly sur-

rounding Pancho, exchanging salutations with him. Arms
and legs edged me out of the picture, but I managed to catch
up with him in the locker room where he sprawled on a
wooden bench and began yanking off his clothes. I tried asking him a question. He didn't hear it. He was pulling his
sweater over his head.

Before I could repeat it, he yelled to the locker room attendant, "Willis—can I have a clean towel?"

He got his towel. I started the same question. Two words
came out when a small boy wandered up to Pancho and
asked, "What do you do with your thumb on the backhand?"

I glared. I knew what I'd like to do with both my thumbs
—something vicious—such as stuffing them into the two
prominent holes in the boy's head. The targets were big. The
holes were wide with hero worship.

Pancho answered the boy who went away happy. I was glad
someone was happy. It wasn't me. Pancho made for the
courts. I followed. I waited three hours and he gave no indication of stopping play. Sun is hot on cement. I'm a perspirer.

I called, "Pancho—when can I get to you?"

He completed an overhead smash and answered, "Be
through in about an hour. Then I'm going bowling. You can
come with me."

I couldn't stand it any longer. I headed for the nearest air-
conditioned bar and ordered a cooling drink. While I sipped
it I opened my notebook and read what I had written today
on Pancho Gonzales.

It was: "Willis—can I have a clean towel?"

Time skipped by quickly while research on Pancho
progressed slowly. Then one day when I was deep in despair
of ever finishing the project, Pancho the unpredictable
pounded on my apartment door and announced:

"I feel like talking."

I certainly felt like listening; and listening, plus talking, proved a successful equation equaling LIFE STORY. While my ancient wire recorder rasped through its longest workout Pancho talked on . . .

Hours later, finished, he said wearily, "Those are more words than I'll speak for the next two years."

I'd be willing to bet my life on that statement.

CY RICE

Introduction

Having toured thousands of miles around the world with Richard Alonzo Gonzales, I probably know him better than anyone with the exception of his mother, father, and wife, Henrietta. I've eaten with him, slept in the same room with him, argued with him, and been beaten on the tennis courts by him.

I still like him.

This is hard to do when a little guy like me continually gets picked on by a big guy like Gonzales. It's always a David and Goliath battle; but unlike the biblical struggle, David has a devil of a time winning.

Playing against Gonzales has improved my speed, sharpened my reflexes. Self-protection is the reason. Otherwise, that power serve coming toward me at 112 miles per hour might knock my head clear back to Ecuador. Spectators can't begin to estimate its unbelievable, blinding speed. You have to face it. The racket in your hand becomes as impotent as a butterfly net trying to stop an atom bomb.

Should you be lucky enough to make a return, a large, blurred image charges the net with the swiftness of a whirlwind and powders the little white ball right back at you, or through you.

Sportwriters have asked me to compare big Pancho's brand of tennis with the greats of yesteryears. I'm too young to do that. It's far easier to rate him with contemporaries—easier because he's head and shoulders above them. Believe me, we who earn our bread and butter in the tennis business are thankful there's only one Pancho Gonzales.

Actually, the only thing I could compare him with are those devastating hurricanes along the Eastern seaboard. There's a difference, though. Weather is fairly predictable.

A lot of people say to me, "You know this guy intimately—what's he like?" Sitting in a comfortable chair I could answer that question in about seventy-five thousand words, but the publishers wouldn't let me because I'm told that's the length of the book.

My only comment is: Pancho's no saint.

But then did you ever see a saint with a tennis racket?

They call him the "bad boy of tennis from the wrong side of the tracks." I don't know what this means. Sometimes my interpretation of the English language is faulty. This I can say, however: One reason I intend taking out my citizenship papers is because Pancho Gonzales is America, and America is Pancho Gonzales. Here is a man who does what he wants to do in a nation where he can do it. He is beholden to no one.

Perhaps I'm not making myself very clear, but after you've read his story and discover what makes Pancho Gonzales play tennis like a demon and run fast through life, you'll understand what I mean.

Francisco Pancho Segura

Contents

15

List of Illustrations

Man with a Racket

1 I Had Arrived

Unzipping the cut-rate drugstore bag, I stuffed in my ninety-eight-cent tennis shoes, my fifty-nine-cent soiled T-shirt, and my rumpled buck-fifty shorts. Then I straightened up and glanced at a mirror.

There stood Richard Alonzo (Pancho) Gonzales. Nineteen years old, six feet three, 183 pounds. Tennis player.

What did I look like? A ferocious competitor? Or a lamb being readied for the slaughter? I had never played in a senior tennis tournament. In fact, there'd been quite a few tournaments I hadn't played in. But now, on that May day, 1947, I had a rendezvous with destiny at the Los Angeles Tennis Club, where the Southern California championships were being held.

I didn't feel like a lamb. Deep inside, something seared me with its white heat. I've heard it described as *desire*. With

me, it was like a pilot light, constantly burning, and neither
bad breaks, missed points nor blind linesmen could extinguish it. That was the only way I knew how to play.

"Richard!" Mom's voice halted me at the front door.

She came from the kitchen, a damp dish towel in her hands.

"You going to the . . . the . . ."

"Tournament, Mom," I helped.

"There will be many people, yes?"

"Sure, lots of them."

"And they'll be looking at you, Richard?" she asked.

I shrugged. "Some of them will, I guess."

"Your clothes are clean?" she asked, eyeing the bag sus-
piciously.

"Yes, Mom, they're clean," I answered, hoping I wouldn't
have to stand inspection.

She studied me for a moment. "You expect to win, yes?"

I said, "Sure."

"If you lose, you won't show your temper before all those
people, will you, Richard?"

"Of course not," I answered quickly. "But I'm not going
to lose . . ."

Mom patted my hand now, like she did so many times when
I was a little boy. "You will not give up this . . . this tennis?"

"Mom, not again," I pleaded, hoping to stave off still another full-scale discussion on the time I was squandering on
the game.

"You know how your father feels about it . . ."

"Yes, yes, I know. I've heard it a thousand times."

Mom sighed and shook her head, and changed the subject.
"You have eaten lunch?"

"I had some beans," I said.

She stood on her tiptoes and kissed me. I left the house.
Halfway down the block I heard Mom's voice.

"Win, Richard!" she called from the porch.

I waved my hand. I would win, I told myself.

I boarded the first of three street cars that would take me within walking distance of the Los Angeles Tennis Club. Riding a street car was sheer boredom—its monotonous speed, the never-changing route. I had a flair for speed and thrills, and I got none of these for my ten-cent fare.

I found a morning newspaper on the seat and quickly thumbed through the pages until I reached the sports section. They'd have my name in the schedule of the day's matches, I thought. I got a surprise. I was in the lineup, sure. But there also was half a column of type building up my second round match with Herbie Flam.

I got the feeling that the interest in "Pancho" Gonzales was not based on what I could do with my racket, but, rather, on what I had achieved off the court—as a non-conformist. I was a curiosity number. Only a few weeks before, when I turned nineteen, my period of suspension by the Southern California Tennis Association had ended. The officials hadn't become softhearted. I simply had outgrown their iron-clad authority over boys of school age. Now I was on my own. Some wondered how I would react.

The story of my suspension had been somewhat distorted in the telling. It painted a picture of me as a "bad boy"—a budding delinquent. The Association had banned me from competitive play in an attempt to rid themselves of the rotten apple that could spoil the rest of the bushel.

Actually, the only offense involved was hooky-playing.

Southern California tennis was ruled by Perry T. Jones. He was major-domo over all U. S. Lawn Tennis Association tournaments in his area; controlled expense accounts of the players; and decided which junior and senior players would be sent to play on the big-time Eastern circuit. Contrary to general belief, I bore no animosity toward Mr. Jones. I had tried to play tennis and play tag with the truant officer at the same time. Mr. Jones had rules, and they were inflexible. It was either attend school or be suspended from tournament play. I refused to go to school. Mr. Jones simply did his duty.

Prior to my suspension, I outranked Herbie Flam in the Southern California Boys' division, having beaten him four out of five times. Herbie was sent East, where he captured the National Boys' championship, while I remained in Los Angeles to continue my battle of wits with the attendance officers. It wasn't an easy game. In fact, I'm sure I covered more ground in one morning than a player would in a whole tournament.

I hadn't played Herbie since 1943, but I knew his game and it hadn't changed very much. Herbie, a well-proportioned boy with crew-cut blond hair, was a favorite of the tennis patrons. He didn't play the so-called "big game." His service was weak, and he never really blew anyone off the court with any of his shots. But what he lacked in power he balanced with his determined, all-court play. He was a speedy, tireless retriever, a superb defender. What I had to do, I was convinced, was to overpower him, particularly on service.

Leaving the third street car, I walked several blocks to the tennis club, showed my player's pass, and entered the grounds. Hundreds were milling about. The men wore smart sports attire and neckties. The ladies flashed the correct afternoon wear. I didn't exactly match their fashion standards. I wore what might best be described as a pair of pants and a shirt—open at the neck. I don't like to button collars, and I hate neckties. They bind me. With this particular shirt, however, I had no choice. It had no button at the collar.

I found not a familiar face as I started for the locker room. Suddenly, there was Herbie Flam, encircled by a group of well-wishers—mostly pretty girls. They smiled at him and appeared to swoon when he spoke. No one smiled at me. No one even talked to me—except one guy I'd never seen before.

Accidentally stepping on my toe, he said, "I'm sorry."

I felt better. Someone had broken the ice.

As I drifted along, I wondered if any of my old friends from Exposition Park would show up. Probably not, I thought. Most of them couldn't get off on a weekday afternoon. Others wouldn't have the money to buy a ticket. Exposition Park was where I had learned my tennis. It wasn't as swanky as the Los Angeles Tennis Club—not quite. It was a public playground with eight hard-surfaced courts, standing in the shadow of the Los Angeles Coliseum. Many Mexicans and Negroes learned the game there. Many others who yearned to play but who couldn't afford even a small fee, watched enthusiastically from the sidelines. Most of us at Exposition Park had two things in common—very little money and a love of tennis.

I dressed quickly in the locker room and found myself more comfortable in my tennis togs when I returned to the crowded clubhouse grounds. I propped myself against the wall of the tennis shop, awaiting the call to the post, and amused myself by studying the crowd and by attempting to pick up snatches of conversation.

As I saw it, the tennis public was divided into two classes. The first group included the week-end duffers—those who played a little and were anxious to see how the better players did it. The other segment was composed of those who were there not to see, but to be seen. The society-celebrity bunch!

I watched the Hollywood movie stars stroll by. Male jaws jutted as smiles flashed on and off. The lovely ladies had much to attract the eye, but I was fascinated by their hair. Almost every color of the rainbow was accounted for, and seldom were there two shades alike. This seemed strange. The women of the race from which I have descended leave their hair as God intended it to be.

In the midst of this amusing exercise, a voice suddenly pierced my thoughts. "Pancho," it came.

I looked up and there were my friends moving in on me. Frank Poulain, who ran the Exposition Park Tennis Shop, which, among other things, was my hideout when the truant officers were hot on my trail; Larry Negrete, my old doubles partner; Chuck Pate, who analyzed the flaws in my game; Fernando Isais, the national horseshoe pitching champion; Arzy Kunz, who operated a tennis shop; David Doughty, leader of the Olympic Tennis Club; and Hubert Scudder, who worked without compensation to develop the tennis talent found in the poor sections of town.

They pounded my back and pumped my hand, and demanded that I blast Herbie Flam off the court.

I nodded, happily. I was no longer lonely.

At match time, I elbowed my way through the crowd, walked onto the court, greeted Herbie and got ready for our warm up. We were on the No. 3 court, right next to the swimming pool. This was mighty convenient, I thought. If I lose, I can drown myself before my buddies have a chance to string me up with the net cord.

The crowd buzzed a little as I gunned my serve in practice. I chased a stray ball near the seats, and as I bent over to pick it up I heard someone in the front row tell her companion, "Look at that scar on his face. It must be a knife wound."

They were referring to my left cheek. No one could miss it.

Today, I'm oblivious to the crowd, but there was a time when my ears picked up everything. I suppose that isn't so strange. Gussie Moran once told me: "I'm conscious of individual faces in the crowd. I remember the same ones from match to match, although I don't know the owners personally." I'm sure Gussie saw expressions on faces that I would never see in my audience. My legs aren't as good as Gussie's —and I've never worn lace on my shorts!

When the match started, Herbie raced through me like he was scheduled to catch a train to Forest Hills. I was overshooting the baseline and missing the sidelines by inches. That's the heartache of tennis—it's a game of inches. Gradually, I began to zero-in on the painted lines, but it wasn't soon enough. Flam wrapped up the first set, 10-8.

My concentration improved in the second set, but so did Herbie's dogged determination. My first service, hit hard and flat, was cannonading off the cement, landing in the extreme corners. Whether it was to Flam's forehand or backhand, it mattered not. I followed it to the net faithfully, hoping to put away a feeble return. But Herbie's returns weren't feeble. Living up to his reputation as a scrambler, Herbie was getting everything back—getting them back and putting pressure on me, to boot. It was very discouraging.

At 5-all, I fell into a streak of inexplicable errors and my touch left me, momentarily. Flam pounced on the opportunity, revved his game into high gear, and moved out in front. To make things worse, he won the next three points on my serve to stand at love 0-4 and match point.

In the meantime, the crowd around our court had become ten-deep, even though Ted Schroeder, the nation's number two player at that time, was performing on the center court. The word of our spirited tug of war apparently had been relayed to the grandstand, bringing hundreds of spectators on the run.

The crowd stood in hushed silence as I started what could have been my last serve. One more point for Herbie and I'd go down the drain. It was too late for planned strategy; too late, it seemed, for prayer. I took a deep breath.

An ear-splitting cry shattered the silence.

"Now, Pancho!"

It was the booming voice of one of my buddies from Exposition Park.

I served an ace.

Again the cry came, "Pancho!"

Another ace.

It was like a battle cry now, and I aced Herbie for the third time.

My confidence returned, but the danger flags were still flying. Twice more Herbie moved to match point, but each time I rallied to deuce the score. Silently, I took up the cry of my friends. "Come on, Pancho." I'd tell myself, "make it good, make it good, make it good . . ."

Herbie scurried for every shot as though his life was at stake, but a well-plastered backhand to the corner was out of his reach. Another deep drive caused him to misfire and I pulled out the game. Ten minutes later, I had the set, 8-6.

I had survived one crisis, but now there was the final set staring me in the face. I paused for a sip of coke and heard a spectator say:

"Look at him! The worst thing he should do when he's overheated."

"Oh, I don't know," another voice suggested. "After all the fiery food he must put in his stomach, it doesn't really matter."

The voices faded out as I forced my thoughts to dwell on that deciding set. Barring a broken leg or an earthquake, I knew nothing would keep me from winning it. My fists clenched tightly as I weighed my desperate mission. It was only a second round match in a sectional championship tournament, true. But to me, at that moment, it might just as well have been the championship for the entire world.

There was no indication that Herbie would run and hide in the third set. He'd be there on the baseline, sending back everything that came his way. He'd battle it every step of the way. He didn't scare easily. And he didn't discourage me, either. In the final showdown, Flam was at his best. But it didn't matter now. My game had answered the call to an all-out attack. I had the shots—the big guns—when I needed them most. And in the end I had the set, 6-4, and the match.

I ran to the net and whacked Herbie on the back, and he smiled and said something kind. And then I sort of drifted off on a pink cloud for a moment to heights that had been unknown to my little world. When I touched down again, I took a solemn oath. I was going to be the best tennis player this game has seen, I told myself. Nothing would stop me now. I didn't care how long it would take, or how bumpy the path would be. I would make it. Damned right I would.

My friends surrounded me now. Quite a few new friends, too. Beautiful girls joined the group—some of the same girls who had been magnetized by Herbie before the match. Everybody loves a winner, I guess.

Leaving the locker room after my shower, a cashmere-coated fellow offered his hand and introduced himself. The name rang a bell. He was a well-known playboy and man about town. He owned a mansion in Bel Air, complete with private tennis court, horses, show dogs, cars, and several mistresses.

"I want you to drop by the house tonight, Dick," he offered.

I said, "What's happening?"

"Cocktail party."

I told him I didn't drink.

He seemed shocked. "Nothing at all?" he asked, incredulously.

"Well, I like a little beer now and then," I conceded.

"Beer? Well, we'll get some. What else do you like?"

I told him I liked beans, and he stifled a laugh.

"Beer and beans . . ." he repeated, pausing as if to double-check his hearing.

The pause told me I wouldn't be heading for Bel Air that night.

"Thanks just the same," I told him.

I felt a touch at the elbow, and a small fellow explained that he was a reporter and had some questions to fire at me. I didn't help him very much and, after a few minutes of "yes" and "no" answers, he looked at me rather hopelessly.

"You don't like to talk very much, do you?" he said.

"Not about myself," I told him.

"You'd better fix that idea," he said, half smiling. "Don't you ever want to be important enough to be misquoted?"

"I just want to play tennis—good tennis," I said with a shrug.

He shook his head and walked away.

Perry Jones stopped me and offered congratulations, and then mentioned that someone was waiting for me in the tennis shop. I went in and encountered a representative of a major sporting goods company.

"How about some equipment, Pancho? What do you need? he bubbled.

"Sure, I need equipment, but I haven't the money right now . . ."

He chuckled and slammed me on the back.

"Who said anything about money?" he roared. "Just call out the size of your shoes, waist, shirt and we'll dig into some of this stuff."

I rattled off the figures for him and soon my arms were filled with an assortment of tennis clothes and two new rackets. I felt embarrassed by his generosity.

"I don't know what to say. What do I have to. . . ."

"Forget it," he interrupted. "You don't have to say anything and you're under no obligation. Now, how're you going to get home with all this stuff?"

"The same way I came, I guess—on the street cars."

He led me outside the club and he whistled for a taxi. He handed the driver a bill.

"Take this gentleman home," he said. "And keep the change."

I jumped into the cab and piled all my new treasures on the seat beside me. The clothes, I quickly decided, I'd give to my brother, Manuel. The rackets I'd take to Frank Poulain, as a part payment for all he'd done for me.

These decisions made, I sank into the cushions, tired, happy. The city streets flashed by. The meter ticked away. It seemed to be clicking out a telegraphic message that I HAD ARRIVED. . . . I HAD ARRIVED. . . . I HAD ARRIVED.

2 The Slums Were Always at Our Heels

I was born in a small apartment near Wrigley Field, which used to be the home of the Los Angeles Angels until the Dodgers headed West. The date was May 9, 1928, which is important only because it establishes the fact that I was a "Depression Kid"—one of the many millions who grew up during our country's most hectic days.

Throughout my early childhood, right up to the day I married, the slums were always at our heels. Mom and Dad would find a neighborhood that was respectably middle-class —a good environment for raising a family. We'd move in. Then, invariably, it happened. Poverty crept in and, in its wake, all the undesirable conditions we were trying to avoid.

"Again," Dad would murmur, as he looked out the window at the disorderly, paper-littered street.

Mom wouldn't reply. She knew what would come next—moving day. Even if we couldn't afford it.

"I don't mind poor people," I heard Mom say to Dad one night. "We're pretty poor ourselves right now, and we don't know what tomorrow will bring. But we do know what's here and it's bad. What kind of children will we raise in this filth and misery?"

So we'd move. And before long, the slums would follow us. It was like a game of tag, and often we became tired of running.

Los Angeles, like any other big city, has always had a serious juvenile delinquency problem. Big cities have slums, and invariably the slums produce many children—restless kids seeking adventure and excitement. In the neighborhoods where we lived at various times, parents had to hold tight reins on their youngsters to prevent them from falling into bad company and all kinds of trouble.

We had few luxuries at our house. Food wasn't abundant, but it was simple and filling, and we never went hungry. Our clothes were just clothes—inexpensive but clean. We wished for many things that never came. And, yet, we were never bitter and we never got into trouble. The reason was simple, I think. My brothers and sisters enjoyed each other's company. Home was a place to congregate. It was something Mom and Dad had drummed into our heads from the day we were born. If you made a friend at school or in the street, you brought him home and he'd become part of the family, too.

My greatest pleasure in those days was to watch a Western movie with a bag full of candy in my lap. This didn't happen too often, which is probably the reason it was such a joy. It's still a favorite pastime. There's only one difference; now I eat the candy more quietly.

I loved beans, milk, oatmeal, salads, and tortillas. Today, money has changed my eating habits. I like beans, milk, oatmeal, salads, tortillas—and *steak!* I never tasted coffee until I was seventeen, and never smoked until I went into the U. S. Navy. Hard liquor meant little to me then—and still does. I like an occasional glass of beer or a vodka drink. My biggest vice not too long ago was poker. But I took the cure one night in a certain California city, where the game is legal, when I discovered that money that comes fast can leave even faster when you're playing with cautious players who can sit and wait for a hand I couldn't.

The poker sessions were a result of the restlessness that constantly gnaws at me. It's as if some giant hand cranks the mechanism of my body too tightly and never lets it run down. I must be doing something every minute of the day, be it tennis, bowling, shooting pool, playing basketball, or driving my "hot rod" wide open. I detest easy chairs, and a bed can claim me only when my body demands sleep. Even at bedtime, I'll take a Western paperback with me and I'll spend the next couple of hours riding the hero's horse.

I've always been this way. As a child, my mother told me to relax. A thousand times a week she'd say, "Sit for a while, Richard." But it was like being sentenced to the electric chair. When my boyhood pals tired of playing games, I wanted to keep going. I remember one boy—the fat boy in our bunch —sitting on the curb, out of breath. "Don't you ever get tired, Dick?" he asked between pants.

I shrugged my shoulders.

"Golly, I think you must have swallowed a Mexican jumping bean," he said, shaking his head.

Maturity, marriage, and fatherhood have had no quieting effect on this desire for perpetual motion. I love my wife and three kids. I like to be with them, but that go-go-go still has me in its grip. Domestication could take place, I suppose, if I broke a leg—or something. Or maybe it will happen when

I reach the age of seventy. Even then, I might take up dueling with canes!

As a youngster, I had no idea what I wanted to be when I grew up. Living near the ballpark, I suppose I might have considered baseball as a career if someone had belted a ball through our living room window. But the Los Angeles club had no sluggers with that much muscle.

I might have become a crooner if it hadn't been for my sister Terry. There was much piano playing at our house, and one day I got up and rumbled a few notes. Terry's hands went limp on the keys. Wheeling on the stool she stared at me, asking sarcastically, "That's singing?" Later my musical efforts were described as sounding like "a pair of kettle drums falling downstairs."

I toyed with the idea of being a professional dancer until the night I took Bertha to a dance and asked her, "How am I doing?"

That old career-busting sister of mine promptly led me to a chair, sat down, removed her shoes, revealing a series of criss-crossed red welts and said, "What do you think?"

I might have gone into the fruit business if the boss I delivered for hadn't fired me for sticking pins into cantaloupes. My motive was unclear. It simply fascinated me to stick pins into cantaloupes.

I do know for certain I never would have become a tennis player if I hadn't wanted a bicycle.

"Too dangerous," Mom discouraged. "You're only twelve. I'll get something safer."

She went to the May Company and bought me a tennis racket. It cost fifty-one cents, including tax.

At first I wanted no part of it. I wouldn't even touch it. "Watch, Richard," Mom said, swinging it wildly and barely missing a statue of St. Anthony.

She extended it toward me, saying, "Here, try it."

I shook my head, backing away a few steps, paling slightly.

"What's the matter, Richard?" she asked.

"A—a cat, Mom," I faltered.

Turning around, her eyes searched the room. "Cat? What cat? Tobey's outside," she said, referring to our household pet.

"The strings, Mom," I said. "Tennis strings come from a cat's gut, somebody told me." I loved cats. Perhaps I'd even known this one.

Mom laughed. "Not a cat, Richard. The strings are silk. The salesman said so."

Reassured, I took the racket and swung it. St. Anthony nearly got it again.

"Not in here, Richard. Take it outside."

I did, straight to a tennis court a few blocks away where I found a beat-up ball worn down to the skin. Standing outside the wire enclosure of the court, I tried bouncing it up and down on the racket surface. Most of the time I missed. When I was lucky enough to make contact, a feeling of triumph and excitement rippled through me. And suddenly I found it challenging.

In the days, months, and years that followed the challenge of hitting a white, fuzzy ball squarely on the strings of a racket grew and grew. Such is the strange hand of destiny.

Undoubtedly the two most significant influences on my early tennis years were Chuck Pate and a Negro youth named Willie. Willie had no hands. How he lost them no one ever knew. No one ever asked him. To me, Willie was the most skilled competitor in the world. He could beat everybody I knew in a game of marbles by using his toes. Willie was an inspiration. When things looked gloomy for me, I'd think of him, and his handicap, and immediately feel better. I never forgot Willie.

Chuck Pate was older. I gravitated toward older companions. Chuck was a fine tennis player, a real student of the game. Why, even today, if something goes wrong with my stroking, Chuck can straighten me out, pronto. The first time he came to our house I wasn't home. Mom didn't know him.

"Is Pancho around?" he inquired.

My mother shook her head. "You must have the wrong house."

Stepping back, Chuck squinted at the number and said, "It's the right house."

Mom said, "No Pancho lives here."

"I'm sorry," Chuck apologized, "but he does."

By this time Mom was becoming a trifle irritated. "Young man," she addressed Chuck, "it's true I have a large number of children. Still, I happen to know all their names. I have no Pancho."

Chuck wouldn't give up.

"Suppose you tell me his last name," Mom said, growing angrier by the second.

"Pancho Gonzales."

Mom's eyebrows shot up. "My sons are named, Manuel, Ralph, and Richard," she said curtly.

"The last one is Pancho," Chuck said.

From that day on the name stuck. Mom fought it, but finally bowed to superior numbers. The official family acceptance came during the finals of a tournament. I was trailing Hugh Stewart and both my parents were in the stands. After a long rally, which I concluded with an overhead putaway, Dad rose to his feet and yelled, "Good work, Pancho!"

When he sat down, Mom tugged at his sleeve. "Did you say Pancho?"

"I said Pancho," Dad replied fiercely.

Mom shrugged. Recognition had been established.

By the time I was thirteen, I was madly in love. It was a

blinding, choking, loyal love filled with devotion and dedication. Obvious to all, it was understood only by a few. The object of adolescent affection was my tennis racket.

My love spread from the first racket to the game itself and its many facets. The love was, and is, undying and possessive. With all due apologies to my wife, I'm wedded to it until old, faltering legs doth us part.

Some might think it strange for an adult to cling so passionately to a sport. I disagree. I'll always remember Roy Campanella's answer when he was asked to describe the key ingredients that make a ball player great. The Dodger catcher, who stands with the best receivers of all time, ticked off "ability," "desire" and some of the other qualifications commonly accepted as essential equipment in the big leagues.

"But, I'll tell you something," Roy added, finally. "I think there has to be a lot of the 'little boy' in a fellow who expects to play baseball the way it should be played."

Campanella's point applies to all sports. The athlete who can approach his game with all the zestful enthusiasm of a "little boy," even when that sport has since become his bread and butter, will always be a tough guy to beat. It's won many matches for me.

That first racket of mine, to me, was the eighth wonder of the world. Loosely strung, producing none of the banjo-like music heard when you twang a tightly-pulled racket of split-lamb's gut, it would shatter today on a second service hit. I never let it out of my sight. I took it to bed with me to protect the strings and a warping frame from the temperature changes of the room. I coddled it like a helpless human. I gave it coats of varnish, and with Mom's manicure scissors clipped the frayed edges of the worn, unravelling strings.

To find the proper grip, Chuck taught me to extend my hand toward it, shaking hands with the handle. I overdid this. I shook hands with it all day, more often than a politician pumps the hands of prospective voters. Sometimes I even talked to it.

I'd say, "Good morning, Señor Tennis Racket."

And, in my own falsetto, the racket would reply, "Good morning, Señor Gonzales."

Then the daily conversation would begin.

"Are you going to be a good racket today?" I'd ask.

"It all depends," came the high-pitched reply.

"On what?"

"The way you use me."

"How should I use you, Señor Racket?" I'd inquire.

"Hit me in the middle. Squarely. Never on the handle. "Never on the wood."

"Anything else?"

"Yes. Also bend your knees. You got to bend your knees. Always."

"Anything else?"

"Face properly. Know where your opponent is."

"Why?"

"So you can hit it where he isn't."

"Anything more?"

"Yes," the racket would reply. "Listen to Señor Pate. He knows. True, I belong to you but he knows me better than you do. He will tell you how to use me."

"Yes," I would answer meekly. "I will do as you say, Señor Racket."

Anyone overhearing this routine might have sent for the man with the white coat. But the repetition of this ritual hammered home the basic rules I learned in practice.

For nearly eight months I hung around tennis courts watching the players—their strokes and maneuvers. All the while I stood outside the wire fences bouncing a ball on my cheap racket for hours on end. Eavesdropping, I learned how to keep score. The painful process took many weeks. It was so illogical and confusing to the child mind. If you scored one point, it was 15-love; two points, 30-love; and three points, 40-love. Somewhere along the line five points were lost.

To this day I haven't found the missing points.

Cropping up frequently as it did in the scoring, the word "love" bothered me. "Zero" or "nothing" seemed like such perfectly fitting words. Why "love," I wondered. The term, "foot fault" was also puzzling. At first I thought it meant a defective shoe.

I had met Chuck Pate while I was attending Edison Junior High School. He was a student at Fremont, and in the afternoon I would watch him practice with the tennis team.

"What's your opinion of the game?" Chuck asked me one day.

Reflecting a moment, I said, "Like it, but . . ."

"But what?"

"Well, it's what everybody says about it . . . you know . . . that it's a sissy game."

Scowling, Chuck spat out, "They're crazy as hell!" Gradually calming he asked, "What sports do you consider rugged?"

I mentioned basketball and football.

"Those are team sports," he snapped. "Tennis is different. You go it alone. No help from anybody. In football the action is concentrated. You wait between plays or after a whistle blows or for a ball to come your way. Tennis has action every second. You've got to make split-second decisions.

"Who's the toughest kid in your school?" he suddenly asked.

I named him.

"Could he beat me in a fight?" Chuck asked.

I grinned. "With one hand. He'd crush you like a tomato."

"Okay," Chuck nodded. "Granted. One thing you don't know, though, is that if he played me a set of tennis I'd have him out on his feet—helpless and gasping—trying to suck air into his lungs."

I'd never thought of this.

"You still think it's a sissy game?" Chuck demanded.

"I've changed my opinion," I admitted.

"You're damned right it isn't," he said convincingly. "It's the toughest."

I was beginning to see the light.

The next four years saw me enrolled at four different high schools. Intermittently I worked, delivering papers from 3:00 A.M., until 8:00 A.M., fought with Dad, and outsprinted truant officers. Tennis was my only reason for ducking school. Once bitten by the bug, the sport ravaged me. And it spread, unchecked, despite Dad's efforts to stamp it out. Prior to that I had been a good student; in mechanical drawing and draftsmanship I was outstanding. But now I wanted no part of school, even though school wanted a big part of me.

My tennis career started inconspicuously. After a little coaching from Chuck, I played my brother, Manuel. He beat me easily. One week later I reversed the decision, playing him left-handed.

Manuel regarded the defeat with amazement. "How come —and not even right-handed?"

I answered his question with a question. "Did you want to win very badly, Manuel?"

He shrugged. "Not particularly."

"I did," I said.

Since that early game with Manuel it's been the same with anyone who ever beat me. I wanted to know why. I went over the matches carefully in my mind, mentally replaying every point remembered. I reconstructed. If opponents had a stroke I didn't have, and it was effective, I copied it to perfection, even tried to execute it better than they had. I borrowed

Jack Kramer's rise hitting, tried Ted Schroeder's looped
cross-court shot, Pancho Segura's volley, and many others. I
borrowed them and I tried to improve them.

School became an increasing chore. How could I listen to a
teacher explaining history when the only history I wanted
knowledge of was tennis? How could I study mathematics
when I only wanted to diagram the trajectory of a tennis
ball in flight? How could I study chemistry when the chemistry in my own body kept urging me to go to a court and run,
run, run?

When I wasn't playing I lolled around Frank Poulain's Exposition Park Shop, soaking up atmosphere and learning the
language of tennis. Ever since Frank took a love set from me,
I hung on his words of advice.

"I've been watching you play and I like you," Frank told
me one day, "because you're a boy who knows how to cry."

"You've got me mixed up with someone else, Frank," I
said. "I never cry."

"To get you mixed up with someone else is impossible," he
replied. "There's only one Pancho Gonzales, remember that.
Never try to be anyone else."

"Okay, but what's this about me crying?"

"You cry," Frank said lightly. "You cry when you lose.
Always."

"Never! I haven't cried since I was a baby," I insisted.

He smiled and said, "Not from your eyes, Pancho. You try
inside. I can't see it happen, but I know it is."

I frowned and became uncomfortable.

"Don't be ashamed of doing it. It's the mark of a champion.
You wouldn't be worth a damn if you weren't bitterly disappointed when you lose."

Frank Poulain is one of the finest men I've ever known.
He's been like a second father to me. Many times I slept on

the old couch in the back of his Exposition Park tennis shop and it was there I found sanctuary when the truant officer chased me. Frank taught me to string rackets, and gave me rackets worth far more than the little work I did for him around the shop.

After several lectures on the value of an education and the importance of finishing high school, Frank threw up his hands hopelessly and said, "I give up, kid. It's no use. I guess you know what you want to do with your life."

I replied, "Yes, Frank. I want to play tennis. Nothing else matters."

"Then play," he advised. "But one thing else—become the best. I think you can do it, too."

My father didn't subscribe to the idea. Although both Mom and Dad were born in Chihuahua, Mexico, they didn't meet and marry until years later in Arizona. They soon realized that, in this country, education is generally the pathway leading to success. They vaccinated my brothers with this thought and it took. With me the verbal needle was sharp enough but my flesh and mind were unyielding.

The inevitable showdown came one night when Dad said to me, "Richard, go to your room."

I obeyed. My brothers and sisters and Mom became silent. I walked into my room, Dad following. He closed the door. I sank into a chair.

"Get up!" he rasped.

I jumped to my feet like a recruit.

Dad is a quiet-mannered man who seldom raises his voice and rarely displays temper. He helps run our family by kindly words, pointing out and encouraging what is right rather than enforcing his wishes by actual commands. It was different now. His patience had left him.

"I want you to have an education!" his voice boomed. I

had never heard him speak so loudly. "I want you to be a fine citizen. I want you to take advantage of the opportunities this country gives a boy. You understand, Richard?"

I signified that I understood.

"You will go to school every day, then?" he asked hopefully.

"I—I can't truthfully promise that, Dad."

His eyes flashed and he bellowed, "Why can't you?"

"Because I have to play tennis," I said. "It . . . it's like it's part of me. Like a leg. Or an arm. It's hard to explain, but I can't give it up."

"I think you will," he said evenly. His eyes focused on my racket and he moved toward it. "This will help you give it up."

Seizing the racket, he broke it over his knee.

"That won't stop me, Dad," I said. "I can get plenty more."

I said it with no feeling of belligerence. I was merely stating a fact. He glared at me.

"You will also give up your friendship with Charles Pate," he said, still operating under a full head of steam.

"Why single out Chuck, Dad?"

"He's a bad influence."

"No. He's my friend."

Dad was adamant. The discussion lasted for over an hour. Mom came in and saw me standing. I must have looked tired for she asked Dad if I couldn't sit down.

"When I'm through with him, not before," he answered. Thirty minutes later he was through with me, but I wasn't through with either tennis or my friend, Chuck Pate.

Dad discovered my affinity for Frank Poulain and his tennis shop and this was the next target. Storming into the shop one day, he announced, "I'm Richard Gonzales' father."

"I'm happy to know you," Frank greeted.

"I doubt if you will be," Dad said abruptly.

Frank came from around the counter and faced Dad. "What's wrong, Mr. Gonzales?"

"Specifically this," Dad replied. "You encourage my son to play tennis. He doesn't need tennis. He needs an education."

"I know," Frank said thoughtfully. "Yet there's nothing I can do. The boy has a strong will."

"I'll break it," Dad said.

"I doubt that you will, Mr. Gonzales," Frank warned.

Dad mulled this over, countering with, "I can try."

Dad started to leave when Frank halted him. "Mr. Gonzales."

Dad turned.

Frank said, "The boy will have made more money from tennis by the time he's thirty than you will make in all your life."

Acting like he didn't believe his own ears, Dad wheeled and faced Frank. "What was that you said?"

Frank repeated his prediction.

"You mean," Dad said incredulously, "that he'll make money out of these?" He pointed at Frank's collection of rackets for sale. "A man makes money from this—this game?"

"The exceptional players do," Frank explained. "And I think your boy's going to be one of the best."

Muttering something unintelligible, Dad left the shop.

He was gradually won over to my side. The process was slow. When full realization came that I was dedicated to tennis, he said to me, "Richard, it seems hard for you to go to all these tournaments on street cars."

"I don't mind it, Dad," I said.

"How do the other boys travel?"

"Mostly in their own cars."

"Then you shall do the same," he said. The next day he

bought an eleven-year-old car for me. I practically dismembered the engine, but when I put it together again not a part was left over. And it even ran better.

It was while I was in junior high school that I won my first tournament, held at the Slauson playground. There were only three entries. With the flip of a coin I drew a "bye," calling "heads" and winning the toss. To this day I still call "heads" if I get involved in any coin tossing and invariably call "rough" when a racket is spun. Heads just seems more important than tails and rough seems to be the treatment I dish out to some opponents.

Anyway, I won the tournament by beating Gene Connors, a man eighteen years older than myself. The third set went to 19-17. My reward was a yellow ribbon and a large chunk of confidence. The ribbon I took home to Mom. The confidence I stored for the future. Bringing trophies to Mom became a habit. Her living room is overflowing, and there's no use planting flowers in them or the family would have to hack its way through a jungle to go out the front door.

Awards I treasure most are the Davis Cup replica of 1949; three sports awards trophies for accomplishment from the *Los Angeles Times,* presented by sports editor Paul Zimmerman and Braven Dyer; and a tiny, battered piece of fast-fading silver won in 1939, at South Park, Los Angeles. The award was for a kid's decathalon—events consisting of paddle tennis against a wall, roque, checkers, caroms, chess, basketball free throws, horseshoes, and ping-pong.

After winning a few boys' tournaments, George Davis, sports editor of the *Los Angeles Herald Express,* mentioned me prominently in a column titled "Southern California—Cradle of Tennis Champions." Frank Poulain clipped the article, slipped it into his pocket and said to me, "Come on, Pancho, we're going to see Perry T. Jones."

"Who's Perry Jones?" I asked.

"Mr. Tennis."

"Pretty good player, eh?" I speculated.

"He was once," Frank recalled. "Now he doesn't touch a racket."

"What's so special about him then?"

Frank tried to explain as we headed toward our meeting with Mr. Jones. He used the terms, "Brass hat" and "bigwig," but I didn't understand them.

Let me digress for a moment. During the last decade it has become a popular pastime to take pot shots at the brass hats of the United States Lawn Tennis Association, either in print or by the spoken word. Frequently you hear those totally unfamiliar with the setup comment: "The boys are okay—it's the brass hats that cause the trouble." Nothing could be more untrue. I ought to know. I caused trouble.

To some of the disgruntled, a brass hat was a cuspidor upside down. To me it was a badge of authority placed on an intelligent head, a symbol of leadership and organizational ability. Somebody had to wear those mythical hats.

Getting back to my trip with Frank, my first impression of the Los Angeles Tennis Club was unforgettable. I'd never seen such a layout. There were tennis courts everywhere and the place had a restaurant, cocktail bar, beautiful furnishings. It had, of all wonders, a locker room. And showers. I couldn't conceive of the luxury of taking a shower anywhere but home after playing. Why there were even two professionals—Gorge Tolley and Loring Fiske.

Frank took me into Perry Jones' office, handed him the newspaper clipping, and introduced me as "the future champion of the United States."

Adjusting his glasses, Mr. Jones regarded me with half-closed eyes. "Maybe," he said after a long pause. And then he quickly added, "That's a long, long road."

"He'll make it," Frank guaranteed.

"I've seen hundreds of promising boys," Jones said. "Most of them fall by the wayside unable to pass the tests."

"Test my boy," Frank encouraged, asking, "You have a test?"

Smiling, Jones removed his glasses, wiping them with a handkerchief. After a full minute had elapsed he said, "There is only one sure test that would work, but human feeling would have to be entirely disregarded."

Frank asked what it was.

"Take a dozen boys up a steep, slanting roof," Jones said with a straight face. "Give them a push. Out of the dozen maybe two would figure a way to get to the ground without being killed. From these two perhaps one would make the grade. Perhaps. He'd already have demonstrated courage, ingenuity, and fast reflexes."

I had been listening carefully, and now for the first time I spoke. "Mr. Jones," I said, "take me to the roof."

He chuckled. "I'm not that inhuman. Let's go to a court instead."

We went to a back court where Mr. Jones found someone with whom I could rally. After ten minutes of hitting balls, he called a halt.

"How's he look?" Frank inquired.

"It's hard to tell," Jones said. "He seems lackadaisical. No incentive."

"That's right," Frank agreed, stating: "but it's true only when he's practicing. He has temperament. He has to have a challenge. When a match counts, he's up. If it's only practice, he's down. If he does well in the Dudley Cup matches," Frank pressed, mentioning the high school tournament, "would there be a chance of sending him East?"

"There won't be any Dudley Cup matches for this boy, nor any Eastern trip," Jones stated with finality.

Before Frank could ask why, Jones said, "I have already

looked up Dick's scholastic record. He's ineligible because he's not in school enough."

"Couldn't something be done to straighten that out?" Frank asked.

"Sorry," Jones said. "A rule's a rule. It's up to Dick to obey the rules."

Riding back with Frank, we didn't talk much. Frank's an understanding guy and he didn't bombard me with questions—only one. He asked, "Made up your mind about school?"

"I sure have."

"What's the decision?"

"I'm finished with school. All I want to do is play tennis. Nothing else. I'll play from morning until night."

Frank sighed and said, "If that's the way you want it, I'll help all I can."

"That's the way I want it," I said.

And that's the way it was.

3 Conquistador

A mindreader with a tennis interest might have been shocked if he'd been able to get a glimpse of my thoughts at the end of the 1947 season. Or, perhaps, he might have gotten a good laugh.

With only one year of senior tennis under my belt, a single thought occupied my mind. "Next year, Pancho, you'll be the national champ," I told myself again and again.

I could put my finger on nothing concrete to back up this optimism. Sure, I'd scored a few good wins. In my first visit to Forest Hills for the 1947 National championships, I had surprised a few officials by knocking off British Davis Cupper Derek Barton, and by forcing third-seeded Gardnar Mulloy to five furious sets before I headed home. And in the Pacific Southwest tournament that followed, I had upset big-name players like Jaraslov Drobny, Bob Falkenburg, and Frankie

Parker before Ted Schroeder shattered my dream in the final. For this, I received a No. 17 national ranking at the end of 1947.

Now, that wasn't bad for a fellow just starting up the road in big-time tennis. But, the fact remained, I lacked the tournament experience that most fellows in the Top Ten owned. A two-year hitch in the U. S. Navy had forced me to tuck away my tennis game in mothballs for most of 1945 and '46 and this, more than anything, threatened to hold up my timetable. A player, aiming at something like the national crown, needs a couple of years on the big wheel in the East—time to adjust to grass surface and the pressure of all-out, day-to-day play.

As I made my plans for 1948, however, I could see no stumbling blocks in the road ahead, but only a big golden throne with me sitting on it. Such is the blind determination of youth. It was this same determination and unwavering confidence that furnished the high-test fuel for the ride to my dreamland.

As the 1948 season got under way, Perry Jones, who sometimes is referred to as "The Emperor Jones," informed me that he would send me East to play on the important grass-court circuit. It is such a decision that pumps fresh life into the heart of an amateur tennis player. In this case it meant that the Southern California Tennis Association would pay my travel and living expenses while I competed in the big events.

This was very decent of Mr. Jones, considering my past suspension. Only a broad-minded person can forgive. He said to me, "Pancho, you're growing up. The circuit will do you a lot of good."

He gave no hint whether he meant my game, my manners or my temperament.

Mr. Jones was right. I was growing up. On March 23, 1948, I had become a husband. When I packed my bags for the

THIS BOOK IS THE PROPERTY OF
THE NATIONAL CITY PUBLIC LIBRARY

Eastern trek, my wife, Henrietta, further underscored my responsibilities by advising me to prepare for fatherhood. It was joyful news, but shocking news, too. An amateur tennis player has a difficult time supporting a wife—especially a player of my standing. What would I do now that we were to become a family of three? The more I pondered this problem the more I realized how well the answer meshed with my dream of tennis grandeur. The national champion wouldn't have trouble supporting a family of three, I mused. The flame within me burned even hotter now.

If I were to ascend the throne at Forest Hills, in September, I gave no indication of it in July, or even August. On the Eastern circuit I rapidly gained the reputation of an in-and-outer. At Southampton, Long Island, for instance, I walloped Budge Patty, the internationalist, 6-3, 6-0, 6-3, but in my next outing I lost to Gardnar Mulloy at Orange, New Jersey. At Newport, Rhode Island, to make my good win over Patty appear even more of a fluke, I fell at the hands of unseeded Sam Match.

I didn't panic, but simply worked on the flaws in my game and trusted I would have the kinks ironed out by the time we reached Forest Hills. In my spare moments, I studied the play of the fellows who loomed at my opponents in the Nationals. I tried to pick out weak spots I might exploit when the chance came, and I filed the data away, mentally, for future use.

The 1948 Nationals stirred up a tremendous amount of interest since there wasn't a clear-cut favorite for the men's singles title. Jack Kramer, after dominating the game throughout 1946 and 1947, had vacated the throne to seek his fortune as a touring professional, and the tennis experts were having a picnic trying to forecast the outcome of the big event.

Ted Schroeder, considered by many as the logical successor to Kramer, held the key to the situation. Since Ted was essentially a businessman and only a part-time tennis player, there was always some question right up to the last minute about Schroeder's plans to play. Ted seemed to enjoy the mysterious role, too.

When Schroeder finally decided he wouldn't compete in the Nationals, the scramble was on. Drobny, Parker, and Tom Brown were given bright chances to cop it all. Billy Talbert and Gardnar Mulloy, a couple of old-timers, couldn't be overlooked. Neither could Bob Falkenburg, who had won in fine style at Wimbledon a few months earlier. Here and there, a kind tennis writer would slip in my name as a "dark horse."

American Lawn Tennis, which was then regarded as the "bible of the game," fanned my hopes with its forecast.

> "Weak from backcourt on the forehand, dynamite at the net, Pancho Gonzales could take it all at Forest Hills this year, provided he hits a streak of hot-hitting that would hold out for the duration of the tournament. It is our opinion that the six-foot-three powerhouse from Los Angeles is one year away from the top. He must not be overlooked, however, for any player who is fast on his feet, continually attacks with accuracy, never knows defeat, and has the faculty for getting the points when he needs them, has the qualities of which champions are made."

I read the writeups. Every guy does, no matter how earnestly some might tell you that they don't. But ever since the time of my suspension for playing hooky, when some writers branded me as anything from a juvenile delinquent up to Public Enemy No. 1, I stopped believing everything I read in the papers. In this case, I found some encouragement from the *American Lawn Tennis* report. They had it figured the same way I did—I had to get "hot" to bring home the big one.

Arriving for the Nationals, I checked in at the Forest Hills Inn—just a block away from the big horseshoe stadium. My accommodations weren't exactly luxurious. Eight of us—all players in the tournament—slept in a room that was intended to sleep but four. Mattresses were placed on the floor for the extras, and I took turns with Hugh Stewart, a fellow Californian, in the rotation between the bed and the floor.

I was strictly on my own at Forest Hills. I had no coach, no advisers. I practised as I pleased and mapped out whatever strategy I thought would be appropriate for a match. The officials paid little attention to me, and only Frank Shields, who later was to become non-playing captain of the U. S. Davis Cup team, expressed some concern over my preparations for the big test.

Observing my lackluster during a workout, Frank came up to me after the session and walked with me toward the clubhouse. Along the way, he told me how important it was to get started in the Nationals with a bang.

"Get the momentum in the early rounds," he said. "Win everything at 6-0, 6-0, 6-0, if you can, for in this brand of competition the 'killer instinct' pays off. It's the only way to keep your game 'up' over the entire ten-day period."

It made good sense, and I thanked him for the advice and promised him I'd be a snarling tiger from the opening gun.

The officials had placed me No. 8 in the seeding—at the very bottom of the list. But I wasn't complaining. I was happy that I had gotten that much recognition—everything considered. Examining the draw, the first few rounds looked easy for me. The battle would shape up in the fourth round. From then on it would be like playing Notre Dame's football schedule—a formidable foe at every stop.

Drawing a first round bye, I got past Ladislav Hecht, the Czech, with no trouble, and then whipped Gus Ganzenmuller in the third round. This steered me smack into left-handed Art Larsen, a fellow who worried me no little. Art was a scrambler, and a good one. And, what's more, he was quite capable of handling all the mustard I could put on my big serve. I sensed trouble.

We started our match late in the afternoon on field court No. 16, and I quickly won the first set, 6-3. Midway in the second stanza, however, the sinking sun, which now had reached a bad angle, began to bother me on the volley. My attack faltered and Larsen was quick to respond to the opportunity. He won the next two sets and I began to wonder if I'd ever get my game going again under those conditions.

During the respite, tournament officials asked Art and me if we'd like to move our match to the Stadium court, which now was vacant. I was too engrossed with my desperate situation to weigh any advantage or disadvantage of such a move. I shrugged my shoulders in reply. Larsen, a guy who always enjoyed the center stage, thought the proposal was a great idea. And so we moved.

It wasn't until we reached the Stadium court that I realized I might escape the tantalizing sun. Now the high, concrete stadium saucer offered me complete protection. I charged to the net again and again with renewed confidence, and my volleying turned the tide in my favor. I won the next two sets, to pull out the match, and I was grateful that Art had made the decision to change horses in midstream.

Frankie Parker was waiting for me in the quarter-final round now, and even though this old hand was top-seeded in the tournament and thirsting for his third national singles title, the situation didn't frighten me. Some of my confidence stemmed from the defeat I had hung on Frankie the year before in the Pacific Southwest tournament, but to prevent myself from getting too cocky I thought of the seventy-five thousand-dollar scare Parker had thrown at Jack Kramer in the 1947 final. Kramer, who was scheduled to accept a fat pro contract upon the successful defense of his title, came dangerously close to losing his crown to Frankie. Jack just did pull it out in the fifth set.

I treated Parker with respect, but midway in the third set I began to think I was home. At that point my game was working like a charm, while Frankie was getting into trouble with his fickle serve and backhand. I won it in four sets.

The excitement at the National championships generally reaches its peak as the play approaches the semi-final round. Our lineup for the run down the homestretch was particularly interesting because it pitted two representatives of what was being called America's "youth movement" against a pair of experienced foreigners. I was to meet Jaroslav Drobny of Czechoslovakia, while my old friend, Herbie Flam, faced Eric Sutgess of South Africa in the other half of the draw. Needless to say, I was pulling for Herbie to come through. What a thrill that would be, I thought, renewing the feud with my boyhood rival right there in the final at Forest Hills! To be completely honest, I must admit that I was giving some thought, too, to the lopsided won-and-lost record I held over Herbie. That, of course, would have made the meeting even more pleasant.

To kill the long hours between assignments on the court, I played cards. Sometimes it was bridge with a handful of officials at the West Side Club. More often, it was a hot game of poker with the players in the locker room. This operation did not produce a profit of any size, but it did keep my mind off tennis for a few hours and gave me a chance to work off my restless energy.

I look back on the 1948 tournament very fondly. I think it was the most enjoyable of all the amateur tournaments I ever played in—not because of anything I did on the court, but mostly because of the friendly atmosphere of the place

—the way so many of the players made me feel welcome. Even the sardine-can conditions of our hotel room provided more merriment than wrangling.

As I dressed for my rendezvous with Drobny, one thought seemed to beat out a tempo through my head . . . "two more to go. . . . two more to go. . . . two more to go."

I pulled the switch. That kind of thinking was hazardous. Throughout the tournament I had been playing my matches one at a time. That's the only safe operational plan in a sudden-death game like tennis. If you don't win today, you won't be playing tomorrow. Now, my thoughts dwelled on Drobny—a left-hander like Larsen—and a tough customer, too.

More than eleven thousand people jammed into the Stadium for the semi-final match. Those who arrived early enough saw Drobny start out as though he planned to run me out of Forest Hills. His southpaw serve gave me fits, kicking, as it did, the "wrong" way. I answered back with all the power at my command and the first set settled down to a battle of serves. It followed this course for seventeen games. In the eighteenth, Drobny cracked through and took the set.

He broke my service again at the start of the second set and opened up a 2-0 lead. Now I began to worry. I played cautiously and drew even, but Drobny was applying terrific pressure. As the set wore on, my serve found the target again and again, and now it was Drobny's turn to fret. And in the turnabout, Drobny's big cannon gave me less trouble. After thirty-seven games, I finally managed to get the lead at 10-9. A passing shot and another ace gave me the set.

I ran ten consecutive points and soared to a 4-0 edge in the third set, and Drobny's game seemed to wobble. At this point, Drobny decided to concede the set and bank on the ten-minute respite to bring him back refreshed. It didn't work.

After five games in the fourth set, his stamina was gone, his keenness was no more. The match was mine, 8-10, 11-9, 6-0, 6-3.

My hopes of meeting Flam in the final were quickly obliterated in the next match, when Sturgess breezed to a straight set victory. Tomorrow I would meet the South African stylist for the U. S. championship. For the first time in the tournament I permitted myself to anticipate the joy of writing my name into everlasting tennis history. Overconfidence would never strike me down now. My thirst for complete success was too great to be denied at this point.

A full house was on hand for the fateful hour. I thought it would never come. A long final in the women's championship, plus a brief summer shower, had delayed the start of our match by almost two hours. There was considerable concern on the part of tournament officials over the possibility of darkness halting our play.

I don't know if the fear of having to wait still another day to fulfill my dream was an influence. At any rate I got off to a winging start against Sturgess and quickly attained my most effective form of the whole tournament. My serve was faithful, my ground strokes strong as I took the first two sets, 6-2, 6-3. Now Sturgess made his determined stand.

In the twelfth game of the third set I stood at match point twice—so near and yet so far away. The first time I hit into the net. The next time I drove over the baseline. The match went on, and now darkness began to envelop the Stadium. After I had cracked Sturgess' service in the twenty-fifth game to move ahead, 13-12, tournament officials came to the court and announced there was time for only one more game. If the match wasn't decided, it would be put over to the next day.

Standing on the baseline, I remembered the proverb of my schooldays, "Never put off till tomorrow what you can do today." I reached back for a little extra power for my serve. My tired legs suddenly had new vigor. The flame within me burned hotter than ever. Within minutes the job was done. Sturgess took my backhand on the half volley and lifted it into the net. Home, at last!

Sixteen months after my first tournament outside the boys' ranks, I had come up smelling like a rose—I was United States singles champion!

American Lawn Tennis trumpeted my victory with this report:

> "The crowd cheered a handsome, dark-skinned Mexican-American youngster who smiled boyishly each time he captured a hard-fought point, kissed the ball prayerfully before a crucial serve, and was human enough to show nervousness as he powered his way to the most coveted crown in the world.

> "Before play began, the experts said twenty-year-old Richard (Pancho) Gonzales was still a season away from the top. Some of the administrative rulers of the American game hoped he would never make it. But Pancho, a player who had to invite himself to important tournaments in order to meet topflight competition, turned out to be the player of the year. Everyone—from the bluebloods to the fans who carried their lunch baskets—seemed to be rooting for the kid from the West Coast. He never let them down."

More important, I didn't let myself down.

4 I Don't Talk Much

Personally, I have nothing against magazine writers, TV and radio commentators, except what they write and what they say. Some, overworking fertile imaginations, have created a fictitious picture of me—the portrait of a Pachuco—a Mexican-American delinquent type, specializing in knifings, thievery, vandalism, disobedience to parents.

This is clear distortion.

A few years ago on a major radio network, a sports commentator whose name is a household one, aired such opinions. Unfortunately, my family was listening. Dad, usually mild-mannered, exploded. Mom started crying. My six brothers and sisters all began shouting at once, pointing at the radio accusingly, just as if the little five-tuber was to blame.

Dad dashed into his room. I waited a few minutes, then followed him. He was bent over a suitcase.

"What are you doing?" I asked him.

"Packing," he snapped, tossing a couple of shirts into the bag.

"Why?"

"Going on a trip." I had never seen him so angry.

"Where to?"

"New York," he fumed. "I'm going to find that lying radio man and beat the devil out of him."

I put my hand on his shoulder. "Listen, Dad. You don't go after nationally-known figures with your fists."

He stopped packing and looked up. "No?"

"No."

"Then I'll take one of your tennis rackets to him."

"Look," I pointed out. "You and I and the family know that what he said is untrue."

Dad didn't answer.

"Don't we?"

He slowly nodded.

"Okay," I said. "What else matters? I don't care what others think. We know. Nothing else counts."

He thought it over and finally jerked his head in agreement, pacified.

Another popular misconception nourished by magazine writers, straining to come up with some sensational copy, was my scar. Around my parents and my own house it was simply referred to as "The Accident." To hear the writers tell it, this scar, which is quite prominent, running from under my left sideburn and ending at the nose, was inflicted during a pool hall fight. Thousands of tennis spectators believe it to be true, because they think a knife scar and Mexican-American youth go hand in hand.

Not only have I never carried a knife, but as a boy I didn't even have a bean-shooter!

The disfigurement happened in 1935. I was riding a home-

made scooter bound for competition in a marble championship. Bill Williams was with me. He was a bigger boy with
longer legs and could push his scooter faster. I was lagging
behind.

"Come on, Dick!" he yelled.

Trying to close the gap, and paying no attention to the
traffic, I got too far in the middle of the street. A car shot by,
the door handle hooking inside my cheekbone, laying it open.
Results: two weeks of hospitalization and a permanent scar.
The car was driven by an off-duty policeman. He was blameless.

A lawyer came over to the house and talked at length with
my parents. Extracting some papers from a brief case, he
pushed them toward Mom and Dad.

"Just sign," he said.

Dad asked for what reason.

"We'll sue and win the case," the lawyer explained.

"No," Mom said, "it was Richard's carelessness. What's
done is done."

The lawyer was not easily dissuaded. His eyes ran over our
inexpensive furniture, took in the many children. "You can
use the money," he pressed.

"Not that kind of money," Dad said, showing him to the
door.

Newspaper tennis writers, ranging from the great Allison
Danzig of the *New York Times* down to sports hacks who
don't know a tennis racket from a snowshoe, have been fair
and factual. When you hit a clean placement there's little
chance of being misquoted.

Still, I can understand the untruths written by magazine
staffers and voiced by radio and TV commentators. I'm a
frustrating guy to interview, mainly because I don't like to
talk much. Certainly not about myself. When I asked Henrietta to be my wife, I cut the proposal down to three words:

"Let's get married." Standing still while being interviewed is harder than beating Rosewall, Hoad, Trabert, Kramer, Segura, and Sedgman on the same day. I'm in one place and I want to be in another—like a bowling alley, or driving my hot rod, or playing snooker. I'm not rude or hard to get along with. I'm simply a guy in a hurry.

Some of these interviewers get more than slightly irritated. An equation forms in their minds: Mexican-American youth, plus scar, equals fight. Sure, I know the American public loves color in their sporting figures and some writers are quite willing to appease the public at any cost—even at the expense of my family. But I don't have to like it.

There was a collection of writers who wore out the phrase that I was "from the wrong side of the tracks." I will go into this later, but if my family was from the wrong side of the tracks, there must be nothing but railroads in the United States.

My early rearing and home environment differed little from that of any boy in an average American home of modest circumstances. There was only one exception. We were left alone every night. It was a necessity. Mom and Dad worked evenings, and also part of the day, to bring in enough money to give us a decent home. We needed no baby sitters. We never admitted we were babies.

I was the boss due to seniority of years, having eleven months on my brother, Manuel. Unimpressed by my age, he wasn't easy to handle. One night when it was time for all of us to go to bed, Manuel refused. He simply shook his head wildly, growling, "No."

I shoved him in the general direction of the bedroom. Staggering a few steps, he straightened up, stiffening like a ramrod.

"You going to bed?" I asked, glaring.

"When I feel like it."

"Do you feel like it?"

"I do not."

"Well," I said, not enjoying the stand I had to take, "I think you better do as I say before you have trouble on your hands."

"I think not," Manuel retorted. His fists were clenched, his eyes blazing. My sisters looked frightened.

I said, "You realize what this means, Manuel?"

"Sure," he returned. "It means I don't go to bed."

"It means more than that," I implied, my eyes straying toward the door.

He knew what I meant. "Let's go," he said, heading for the back yard.

We went outside. I hated to do it. We were very fond of each other. But my position as head of the children was in jeopardy. I couldn't allow my authority to be challenged.

It seemed like the fight lasted an hour. Neither of us got hurt. Actually, it was mostly wrestling and pulled punches. The other children were horrified onlookers. Manuel finally ran out of breath. We were both glad to go to bed.

We had several more fights from time to time, but this was the only fight I ever won. Manuel developed a system. He would hit me and run. I couldn't catch him.

Some reporters have compared me with a cloak and dagger operator simply because I don't like to talk much. I learned years ago that the man who listens never makes a fool of himself. Switching a couple of proverbs—to me, deeds are mightier than words, and the racket mightier than the pen.

Some years ago I knew a businessman who had occasion to send many telegrams. One day I noticed that within fifteen minutes he dispatched two short wires to the same man.

I inquired, "Forget something important in the first wire, George?"

"No," he said, smiling sheepishly, "I figure you can't be illiterate in ten words."

Talking tires me more than a long set. I'll leave it to the politicians. Only once in the course of my entire life can I remember really enjoying talking, and this was on the telephone. The rare occurrence followed the 1949 doubles finals in the Southern California Tennis Championships. It was a marathon match, the longest in American, and possibly world, tennis history. The four tired participants were Gonzales and Hugh Stewart vs. Ted Schroeder and Bob Falkenburg. The match lasted five hours and twenty minutes.

Schroeder and Falkenburg won, 36-34, 4-6, 3-6, 6-4, 19-17.

Hundreds of spectators sat without dinner, the final point being scored at 9:00 p.m. The crowd was chilled. It had been a balmy day, but after the sun dropped from sight the temperature fell about twenty degrees, catching the fans with insufficient clothing.

At the finish of the match I went into Perry Jones' office and sat down at his desk to tackle a big, thick steak that a kind woman who lived near the Los Angeles Tennis Club had cooked for me. Every time I took a bite the telephone rang and somebody wanted to know the final score. I obliged, although the steak got cold.

Mr. Jones came in and saw me trying to eat and talk into the phone at the same time. "You don't have to answer it, Pancho," he said. "Go on and eat your dinner."

"But I want to, Mr. Jones," I insisted.

"Why?"

"Well," I explained, "it's the first time I've ever felt like an executive."

Even after I won the Nationals at Forest Hills in 1948, I didn't feel like talking. While still soaking wet with perspiration, I was hemmed in by reporters. The barrage of questions began. There was no escape.

"How does it feel to be champion of the United States?" I was asked.

"Fine," I said.

"Got any plans?" came from another.

"None."

"What's the first thing you're going to do now that you're the champ?"

"Take a bath."

"Are you considering turning professional?" was the next question.

"Hadn't thought of it."

"Whom do you credit with the development of your game?" a squeaky voice shouted.

"Myself," I said.

Henrietta pushed through the crowd and threw her arms around me. We kissed. "Darling, you were wonderful," she said.

My shirt was sticking to me like glue. "I'm going to get you all wet," I told her.

"Who cares," she said.

I edged toward the clubhouse, holding her hand. I saw a slight clearing near the entrance and pulling her by the hand I broke free from the mob and made it. I had something on my mind. As a matter of fact, it began preying on my mind the moment the match was over. I had to do something about it.

I wanted to ride the roller coaster at Coney Island.

5 The Honeymoon

When I first laid eyes on Henrietta Pedrin, my old black dog, Butch, was the only one to notice the chemistry change taking place within me. When she walked into my house I had been slapping Butch rather roughly on the rear. After taking one long look at this small, dark, seventeen-year-old girl, the hand pounding Butch became gentle and began stroking with affection. The dog couldn't quite understand what was happening, and maybe I couldn't either. All I knew was that when I looked at her and tried to swallow, something like moons and stars seemed stuck in my throat.

Henrietta was one mess of a name, I thought, and if I shortened it to Henry, the connotation didn't do justice to ninety-eight pounds of softness. Later on I might think of a more fitting name; that is, if I ever saw her again. Somehow I thought I would.

I'm supposed to inform the readers of my love, my courtship, my honeymoon. A woman remembers these graduating stages better than a man. She recalls what she expected and what she got—or didn't get. I have a knack of squirming out of things, and here is a good opportunity to turn over this part of the story to the girl I married. So let my wife speak.

When I first met Richard in 1948, my hair was coal black, and still is, but how much longer I can keep it from turning gray depends on how much longer my husband races his hotrod. His excuse is that the children are crazy for the trophies he brings home. All I care is that he brings himself home—in one piece.

Richard's sisters, Margaret and Terry, had invited me to the Gonzales house to a party. I went with a boy friend. I was introduced to Richard, who was sprawled on the floor petting a black dog. They said he had just returned from playing in a tennis tournament in New Orleans. I knew nothing of tennis.

Stacked in a corner of the room were a lot of silver trophies. I examined them. They were not engraved, and I couldn't understand why. I remarked to Richard, "Why isn't any writing on those cups?"

He scrambled to his feet. He certainly was tall. I'm only five feet, one inch. When he spoke his voice seemed to float down from the ceiling.

"Engraving costs money," he said solemnly. "We don't have much money around here."

I nodded. I understood. I had grown up under the same conditions. "But," I asked, puzzled, "how do you remember where you won each one?"

"That's easy," he said. "Tennis players are like elephants. They never forget."

"I never met any tennis players," I told him.

"Well, have you ever met any elephants?" he joked.

I shook my head.

"Well, at least you know a tennis player now," he said, dropping back to the floor and flea-bitten Butch. And that summed up our entire conversation during the first meeting. One particular thing stuck in my mind: the way he flopped on the floor. It reminded me of a graceful parachute landing.

He called me the next night and without wasting a single word asked, "Can I have a date?"

I said, "When?"

"Tonight," he answered.

I was slightly surprised. At the party he seemed disinterested. "Well . . ." I hesitated.

"Harry James is at the Aragon Ballroom in Ocean Park," he announced. "You like to dance?"

"I love to."

"I'll be over at eight-thirty," he said.

I said, "Not so fast. I'll have to ask mother."

Mother knew of the Gonzales family and consented. Promptly at eight-thirty Richard appeared in an old beat-up Ford that ran like a new car. He'd completely overhauled it. He drove fast and talked little. I didn't talk much either. It's hard to talk with your heart in your mouth, and that's exactly where mine was as Richard snaked through the traffic.

When we went into the Aragon he said, "I used to be a lousy dancer, but I'm okay now."

"You'll have to be," I said, doing some rapid calculating. "You're at least a foot taller than I am."

He laughed. "Down on the floor our feet are even. The other end doesn't count."

"The other end," I said, "will hardly be visible."

A few steps later I knew that he was an excellent dancer with perfect rhythm. I strained on my toes trying to grow a few inches, to make it easier for him. During the intermission

I parked my shoes in a safe place and danced in my stockinged feet on top of his feet.

We were having a soda and he said abruptly, "What about the boy who brought you to my house?"

I glanced up at him. "What about him?"

"You in love with the guy?"

"Nope."

"You in love with anyone?"

"Not even myself," I replied.

"Good," he said. "Let's dance."

The next day he telephoned for another date. "You're so light on my feet," he laughed, "let's do it again."

I said, "I don't mind being on your feet, but not at your feet."

"What's that mean?"

"That means I'm no hero-worshiper," I said. "I've heard a lot about your tennis. It doesn't mean much to me. It's the boy without the racket that counts."

After a moment of silence, he said, "Does your mother like me?"

"Sure. Why?"

"No reason," he said. "Pick you up at the same time tonight."

This was the beginning. With every date our mutual interest mounted. For two months we went steady, afternoons and evenings. Often in the afternoons I'd sit around the Exposition Park courts watching him practice. He handled his body beautifully. He had natural grace. He had a fierceness too—the way he smashed at the balls.

The next tournament on his busy schedule was at the La Jolla Beach and Tennis Club. La Jolla is a resort town near San Diego. I understand it compares in beauty with the French Riviera—blue waters, white beaches, curving coastline, mountains rising sharply behind the city. Richard wanted me to go with him. This would mean staying overnight. He said he'd made arrangements for Beverly Baker, now Beverly Baker Fleitz, an ambidextrous, highly-ranked player to room with me. Richard's brother Manuel was also going along. Mother was won over after I satisfactorily answered a few questions.

Richard failed to win the tournament but he won me, and I agreed to go to Yuma and marry him. Manuel would accompany us. Marriages were fast in Yuma, Arizona, and Richard enjoyed anything that was fast.

We decided to keep our plan quiet. Richard said his folks would never give us their blessing, believing marriage at this particular time injurious to his tennis career. My own mother would never approve and I could almost hear her words, "A girl of seventeen doesn't know her own mind." I may have been a teenager, but I knew my mind. It was made up. Nothing could sway my decision. I wanted Richard.

I lay on my bed the night before the big step and thought it over. I am sure that most girls contemplate a slow domestication of their husbands that finally results in complete control. I held no such ideas. I knew I could never handle Richard unless I used an electrically charged chair—the kind a lion tamer uses. Furthermore, I knew I could never completely own him, and the best I could expect was to share him with tennis. If I could compete with only one tennis court I might have the upper hand. But there were hundreds all over the world and only one Henrietta Pedrin. I shrugged it off. Don't fight it, I thought—join it.

The next day we raced toward Yuma. I wanted to fool myself thinking, "He's burning up the highway for me . . . breaking speed records to get married." I knew differently. Speed and Richard were twin brothers.

After the secret marriage, I returned to my house and Richard to his. He hid the license in a desk at his house. I hid my wonderful feelings and emotions at my house. Our parents suspected nothing.

One night Richard called for me, and Mother greeted him with her arms folded across her chest. I knew the pose. Formidable!

"Henrietta stays home tonight," she stated.

"Why?" Richard asked calmly.

"Because," Mother explained, "she's too young to be going out every afternoon and night."

I didn't intervene. I was curious to know how Richard would handle the situation. I could see he was angry.

"Have you any personal objections to me?" he asked Mother.

"None," Mother answered. "It's . . . it's just that she goes out too much."

Richard put his hands on his hips facing Mother. He was boiling inside, and I hoped that he'd contain himself. I hate scenes.

"Mrs. Pedrin," he said, "the law's on my side."

"Law," Mother repeated. "I don't know what you mean by that, young man."

"I mean," Richard said very deliberately, holding his anger in check, "that a married man has the right to take out his own wife."

I gulped. Mother's face blanched. She groped for a chair.

"It's true," I said, and I started explaining, fast.

Before we had a chance to tell his parents, they found our marriage license quite by accident while they were going through the contents of the desk. Everyone knew now. It was better this way. For the first time I had the feeling of being married. We rented a small apartment and began to live a fuller life.

Nearly every morning Richard was off to practice tennis. I wasn't jealous or felt neglected. My own hopes were tied up in his life's work, and his life's work was tennis. We were dependent upon it for income, even though he was an amateur. Expense money for tournament travel can be stretched. We were just squeaking by.

Richard had shortened my name to Henry. "It doesn't fit you," he had said, "but it's the best I can do."

"Henry," he reminded me one day, "we never had a honeymoon."

"It can wait," said the economical wife.

"No," he said impulsively. "We've got a couple of hundred. Let's go out and spend it."

I didn't argue. No girl can turn down a honeymoon, even a late one. We packed old clothes. I knew better than to pack any fancy ones, being married to a guy who thinks he's going formal if he wears a necktie.

"We're going up the coast," he informed me. I didn't care where we went. Just having him to myself was enough.

The second day of our trip, the scenery was startlingly beautiful, the highway curving around solid hunks of mountain. Far below were boulder-strewn beaches. We caught up to a station wagon, loaded with camping equipment, bearing green Vermont license plates. It was traveling at a moderate speed.

Richard began to fret. He couldn't pass the car because there were no cutouts, no straight stretches and no side roads. For ten minutes he said nothing. Finally he grunted, "I don't want to spend our honeymoon breathing gas fumes."

"Drop behind," I advised.

Taking his eyes off the curving road, he fastened them on me. I should have known better than to suggest retreat to *him*.

I looked at the sky. It was a reminder of Richard's face— a massing and curving of black, spiraling storm clouds. Rain was in the air. I could almost smell it. We zipped around another mountain, close to the perpendicular cliffs. Here the road ahead was visible for nearly five miles—five miles of twists and turns, skirting more mountains, broken here and there by a few canyon mouths.

Richard swore softly. The oath was mild enough, but he suddenly remembered me and said, "Sorry."

Two more miles curved by and then suddenly Richard raised his arm, pointing excitedly, "A road, Henry! In the canyon!"

I saw it, a thin, wavering ribbon of dirt that vanished from sight under a thick covering of leafy trees. The map was on the seat and I reached for it. A few seconds of scanning and I reported, "Not on here, Richard."

He paid no attention. His eyes burned brightly, and color crept into his cheeks. Even his breathing was faster, and his hands gripped the steering wheel hard.

"It isn't on the map," I repeated.

"It's a short cut, Baby," he said. "My sense of direction tells me this road'll bring us back to the highway." I let him talk on. "Probably lots straighter, too. When it hits the coast again, the station wagon'll be behind us. Can you imagine the face of the driver, Henry?"

"Please, Richard," I protested gently.

He patted my knee. "Wait and see," he said.

I sighed. He swung the car sharply, treading the smooth asphalt for dirt. The road was bumpy. Behind us trailed dust.

I heard a strange noise; like something following us. It was rain, torrents of it coming over the trees as if searching for our car. When it caught us, Richard slacked his pace, starting the windshield wiper. After a few seconds of hesitation, it began working.

"Scared?" he asked me.

"No," I lied, twisting a handkerchief between my fingers. It always helps.

Night was coming, and the tall trees hurried the disappearance of day. Richard flicked on the headlights. The rain had stopped falling, and assorted puddles glistened under the dancing car lights.

"Hungry?" he questioned.

"A little."

Five minutes later he squinted through the streaked windshield. "A light. Down the road."

I saw a faraway electric blur that gradually merged into a sign of four letters—"FOOD". The building was a simple roadside shack, small and unpainted.

Richard braked to a stop. "Let's try it," he said.

We went in. An old man with a stubble of ragged, red whiskers snapped off a static-filled radio and greeted us.

After we ordered, and the hiss of frying hamburgers and the tempting aroma of onions filled the shack, the proprietor turned from the grill, asking, "You folks heard the news?"

"We haven't heard anything but rain," I said.

The old man brought the hamburgers and milk to the counter and took his time before answering. When he got around to it, he said, "Landslide above the coast highway. Knocked a car plumb over the cliff into the ocean. Heard it on the radio."

"How awful," I said.

"Yes," the old man continued, "terrible thing. Big station wagon. Two got killed."

I stopped eating. Richard kept on but he chewed very slowly. "Did . . . did the car have Vermont license plates?" I asked, and my voice trembled.

The old man eyed me closely and scratched his head. "Yep, it *was* a Vermont car."

We didn't talk about it. When Richard paid the check, he inquired as to the fastest way to the coast highway.

"Take the right fork at the top of the hill," the old man said.

We climbed the hill, and at the crest our lights picked up the intersection. Richard slowed the car. His voice vibrated with excitement as he said, "I think the left road is a short cut."

"Yes, Richard," was all I said.

I believe this story furnishes you with a true picture of Richard and the way he reacts. Believe me, it's never dull married to a man like this. It's much like living with a ball that never stops bouncing. He has, I admit, changed a little since we were first married. He's not as carefree. A few years ago when he crossed a street he scarcely glanced at approaching cars, almost challenged them to hit him as he swaggered along. Now he looks.

Not long ago he was talking in his sleep, something he seldom does. He usually sleeps like he's dead. I woke him up because he seemed unhappy and asked what he was dreaming.

Snapping on the bed light, he peered at me long and earnestly. "Why are you staring at me?" I asked, minus my makeup.

He grinned. "You don't look a bit like him," he said mysteriously.

I sat up. "I hope I don't look like any him."

"I was dreaming the truant officer was chasing me," he said. "The funny part of it was he looked just like you."

I didn't think it was so funny. Subconsciously he was realizing the responsibilities of life. These things come hard for Richard.

I try to be a good wife. The main thing is to give him complete freedom and keep out of his hair, never saddle him with a problem, leave his mind free to concentrate on being the best tennis player in the world. Staying out of his hair is easiest of all. He doesn't light in one place long enough.

Of this I am sure: I married a tornado. But I wouldn't for all the world trade him for a zephyr. Richard is Richard. Wild, almost like an animal, always running somewhere after something. The formula for holding such a man is to throw away the leash.

Once I heard a radio funnyman describe a well-matched couple. "They fight to a draw every night," he quipped.

By these standards, Richard and I are misfits. We don't fight. You can't fight with perpetual motion. Somebody has to stand still for a minute.

I guess it's better this way.

6 All's Well That Ends Well

I didn't expect the whole world to change suddenly when I became National champion. Frankly, I didn't know what to expect. My dreams usually took me to the point where I was tossing my racket high in the air in triumph. That was as far as they'd go—and that had always seemed far enough. What more could a guy ask of a dream?

I came to be thankful that my dreams had always stopped at that point. If I had expected the world to become something like Alice's Wonderland once the title was mine, the letdown that followed might have been even harder to have endured.

To be sure, the days immediately following my victory in the 1948 championships at Forest Hills were crammed with excitement and many "first time" thrills. And for a time it seemed certain that my world would always be bright and totally beautiful. My picture was on the front pages of newspapers from coast to coast. Sports writers hailed my somewhat sudden "arrival" as the dawn of a new era for tennis, predicting that I would eventually lead tennis back from the graveyard. I was wanted for television shows, radio interviews, magazine articles. I was the "kid from the other side of the tracks," as they put it, who had barged into the sweet-smelling game of tennis and had taken it for my own. And everybody loved me for doing it!

It didn't take me long to learn the hard facts of life—that the fellow on top has no place to go but *down*. When a champion wins a good match he gets a shrug of the shoulders. Champions are supposed to win. But when he loses, well, that's something else. He's a bum. It's a simple pattern and I suppose it applies to most American sports. However, as a twenty-year-old come-lately from Exposition Park, I found the fickle affection of the gallery and press quite confusing.

My California friends really whooped it up for my homecoming from Forest Hills. The sports writers, in the meantime—Mel Gallagher, Bion Abbott and Luipi Saldana—were stirring up excitement over the possibility of a Gonzales-Schroeder match during the playing of the Pacific Southwest championships—the tournament that traditionally follows the big show at Forest Hills.

"A match with Ted Schroeder," one scribe pointed out, bluntly, "would soon let us know the real worth of our new National champion."

I could hardly disagree with him.

Schroeder was recognized in most tennis circles as the uncrowned king of the American courts. He had not attempted to put an "official" stamp on this reputation by playing in the National championships. His business interests prevented this, although he did have time to compete in the

Davis Cup Challenge Round, which had been staged at Forest Hills a few days earlier. But it never seemed to matter whether Ted played or not; many tennis observers—especially those in high, official places—felt that Ted could be champ if and when he felt like it.

Winning the title at Forest Hills had given me a tremendous shot of confidence, but I had to wonder how much this would help me when I faced Schroeder across the net. I had never been able to beat the guy. Jack Kramer sums up Schroeder's strange hold on me in one, brief sentence: "Ted simply was a better player."

I don't agree.

Ted held some kind of psychological advantage over me. I was never able to understand it. I still can't. He'd get me worried long before a match started. Often as we dressed in the locker room, he'd approach me and the conversation would run something like this:

"Hello, Pancho."

"Hello, Ted."

"Good day for tennis."

"Yeah."

"You know, I'm going to beat you again, Pancho. . . ."

Then he'd stroll away, as nonchalant as ever. I'd stand there and burn—playing right into his hand. He was halfway home before we'd even hit a ball!

Chuck Pate helped me analyze Ted's game. Chuck did a great job. He spread out all the details on a table top, and everything made sense. It was like handing a fellow the combination to a safe—but I still couldn't open it. There was no doubt about it, Schroeder was my jinx.

Ted played almost daily at the Los Angeles Tennis Club. For a period of about a week, he didn't show up at all. This seemed strange.

"Where do you think Ted is these days?" Chuck inquired.

"He's probably at home—practicing," I said.

Chuck looked at me, puzzled.

"Practicing—at home? How'd he do that?"

"Not on a court—on a doll," I explained. "He's got a doll that looks like me, and he's sticking pins in it. You know, black magic!"

Chuck smiled weakly.

"Don't let the guy get you down," he warned. "You'll catch up with him one day."

I wanted to catch up with him in the Pacific Southwest. That would give me a season I could really celebrate—the National championship, and my first win over Schroeder. Wow! The thought flashed through my head like a beacon all through the early rounds of the tournament. It'll be different now that I'm the champ, I promised myself.

Evidently, Ted hadn't heard about me winning the title. If he had, he remained unimpressed. When we got together in the semi-final round, before a packed house at the Los Angeles Tennis Club, he showed no respect at all for the new crown that had been placed on my head. And it was like old times.

It was a slam-bang, gallery-pleasing match all the way. At one stage, in the fourth set, I came within a point of tying up the match, but they don't pay off on "almost." When the final returns were in, Ted had the match, 6-3, 4-6, 7-5, 10-8. My title seemed a little tarnished now.

But that was only the beginning!

The following week, in the National hardcourt championships at the California Tennis Club in San Francisco, Ted again demonstrated his supremacy. This was a particularly bitter pill. A victory in the hardcourt event would have given me a grand slam of U. S. outdoor championships, since I already had won the clay and grass court titles in '48. But it was Ted who added to his glory. This time he breezed to a 6-4,

4-6, 6-3, 6-1 victory, running his winning streak over me to
seven straight.

Two successive losses in the first month of my reign! What
a disgrace, I thought. The next time out, however, my neck
got even redder. Playing in the semi-final round of the Pan-
American championships at Mexico City, I dropped a quick
11-9, 6-0, 6-4 decision to Eric Sturgess—the same guy I had
beaten in the Forest Hills final.

Now the tongues really began to wag. Some began to
chant that my title win was a fluke. Others said I was still a
year away from becoming a winning player. I wasn't in a
position to argue.

There was some speculation that the U. S. Lawn Tennis
Association would break tradition and by-pass me for the
Number One rung in the 1948 national rankings. The top
spot almost automatically goes to the national champion,
but considering my spotty record and my inability to beat
Schroeder, it was suggested that, perhaps, Ted belonged at
the head of the parade. When the lists were published, however, the Association placed me at Number One; Ted, at
Number Two.

This confidence in my Number One spot, I believe, helped
me achieve what had loomed as the impossible. Playing in
the La Jolla Beach Club Invitation tourney, I finally got
around to beating Schroeder, but even then I had to do it the
hard way.

On the eve of my match with Ted, my doubles partner,
Hugh Stewart, came close to spoiling my hour of triumph.
Hugh's a big guy, with a strong overhead. In the middle of a
doubles match, he drifted out of position on a high lob. Just
as I was about to swing at the ball, Hugh's racket came down
on the bridge of my nose. An explosion took place inside my
head. Blood spurted. The match ended and I was rushed to a
doctor.

"It's broken," the doc informed me, as he worked it back into place.

"Can I play tomorrow?" I asked, thinking of my date with Schroeder.

He shrugged. "It's up to you. You won't be comfortable. You'll have to breathe through your mouth."

The tournament chairman expected me to default because of my injury. That night I called him. "The match is on," I told him.

The next afternoon, with my swollen nose taped and my head still a little numb from anaesthetics, I played the best tennis of my life. I beat Ted, 6-2, 6-8, 9-7, and at the end of the match I felt like a new man.

"I'll gladly break my nose every day of the week if I can be sure I'll play as well as I did today," I told reporters.

The victory made the score 7-1 in my personal duel with Ted. It was still a bit lop-sided, true, but at least I had broken the ice. The next time it would be easy, I told myself.

But it wasn't. In our very next clash, Schroeder gave me the worst beating ever—6-1, 6-0, 6-2, and, what's more, it took him only forty minutes to wrap it up.

I had started 1949 with two big goals in mind—to win at Wimbledon on my first trip abroad, and then to defend my title at Forest Hills. This was the combination I needed to become a sound prospect for a pro tour, and, of course, a big-money tour was the answer to all my other problems.

I had launched my program nicely enough by winning the National Indoor championships in New York, beating Billy Talbert, one of the finest players on boards. The metropolitan newspaper and wire service writers agreed that I had the knack for winning "the big one." I wanted to believe them, but in the months that followed, these writers, along with many others across the land, changed their tune.

At the River Oaks tournament in Texas, in April, I suffered a terrible loss at the hands of Sam Match. Sam blistered me in twenty-eight minutes. In the French championships at Paris, I was drubbed by Budge Patty. In my debut at Wimbledon, Australian Geoff Brown put me out in the third round. The tide turned, temporarily, when I returned to the States and successfully defended my National Clay Court championship against Frankie Parker. But when I checked in for the all-important play on the Eastern, there were few winners in my racket.

Billy Talbert knocked me out at Spring Lake, New Jersey, and again at Southampton, Long Island, where we staged a grueling five-set final. On the plus side, I downed Vic Seixas for the Pennsylvania grass court title, and won from Gardnar Mulloy in four tough sets at Newport, Rhode Island.

It was mid-August now, and the Davis Cup Challenge Round and the National championships were only a couple of weeks away. I needed time. I needed it desperately. My game was coming along—sharpening with each tournament. I had that feeling in the finale with Talbert at Southampton. And when I followed with wins over Seixas and Mulloy, I knew I was getting closer to the target. But was it the right timetable? Would I be prepared for Forest Hills?

My two singles matches in the Challenge Round, in which I defeated Frank Sedgman and Billy Sidwell, contributed two points to our 4-1 triumph over Australia. But they did more than that for me. The keen competition of Cup play was just what the doctor ordered for my game. I knew I was ready to put my crown on the line.

On the eve of the 1949 Nationals, however, there weren't too many tennis observers who gave me a chance. Tennis expert John M. Ross, writing in *Sport Magazine*, summed up the situation without pulling a punch:

"It has been a full year since young Richard (Pancho) Gonzales, the problem child of tennis, stood the net world on its ear with his awesome surge to the top rung of the amateur ladder. But most tennis addicts still have not recovered from the shock—not even Pancho himself.

"The unprecedented havoc wreaked by the dazzling Californian in last year's Nationals was branded at the time as a fluke by some, and a catastrophe by others. And, in the intervening months, his fickle form has not only glorified his critics, but has earned for him the rather ignominious accolade of 'cheese champion.'

"When Pancho struts across the turf in this year's edition of the Nationals at Forest Hills to protect what's left of his somewhat battered crown, he will be standing at the crossroads of his brief and hectic career. If he can duplicate his 'miracle of '48,' there will be a pot of professional gold waiting at the end of the rainbow. But, if he fails, he may never hear the knock on the door again.

"Not many tennis players have encountered such a crisis at the tender age of twenty-one."

Ross was right; it was a crisis, indeed—a seventy-five-thousand-dollar crisis. And it was a crisis I had created through my own mistakes. I can't honestly say that the national title went to my head—it wasn't quite that bad. But I know I didn't train as hard as I did when I was gunning for the championship. My next mistake was restricting myself to only local tournaments for about six months. This combination caused me to blow up to 208 pounds—about twenty-five pounds over my normal playing weight.

But even the knowledge that my problems were created by my own mistakes did not comfort me. It didn't make it any easier for me to read what the tennis writers were saying about me. The same fellows, who only a few short months before had labeled me as "the boy wonder," suddenly changed the tag to "cheese champion." The brand followed me everywhere and added to the pressure of trying to get into shape while playing in important torunaments.

Although the newspaper blasts hurt me deeply, they also made me more determined than ever to land on my feet. But this wasn't the only factor behind my late-season push. There was the matter of Ted Schroeder. Our showdown was at hand.

Ted was in the process of establishing himself "officially" as the best tennis player in the world. He had won the Queens tournament in London, and had followed this with a spectacular triumph at Wimbledon. He ducked the Eastern grass court circuit, but in the Challenge Round he won two matches, running his streak to seven consecutive Davis Cup triumphs. Now he figured to finish in grand style by copping the Nationals.

Bobby Riggs, who at that time was in control of the big-money pro tour, had designated Schroeder as his next headline attraction, and was planning to pit Ted against Jack Kramer, the newly crowned king of the pros. There was only one hitch in the plan—Schroeder had to beat me. And I had some ideas of my own concerning the identification of Kramer's next opponent on tour. It mattered not that the record book showed Schroeder owned me. He'd find that snatching a potential seventy-five-thousand-dollar pro contract from my grasp wouldn't be like taking candy from a baby.

The tournament officials added a little fuel to the fire that now was burning within me by designating Schroeder as the number one seed. I got number two. That was sort of an official confirmation of what everyone was saying. I didn't complain. Nor was I bitter over the way the tennis brass had rallied to Schroeder's side for the showdown. Almost to a man, the officials were pulling for Ted. He was their kind of guy—

personable, poised and a good talker. To underscore how
they felt about him, U.S.L.T.A. officials gave him the William
Johnston Trophy during the tournament, an award that
stresses "character, sportsmanship, manners, cooperation, and
contributions to the growth and development of tennis."

To make sure I had at least one supporter in the gallery, I
brought Henry to Forest Hills with me. Our little boy, Richard, Jr., while a Gonzales fan, remained with his grand-
parents in California. I had to wonder, as the tournament
progressed, if I had made the right decision in letting Henry
come. Henry was pregnant, and the ever-increasing tension
of our most important hour was not conducive to her well-
being. My wife, you see, becomes very emotional during my
matches.

When we arrived at Forest Hills I shied away from all
invitations to parties and the like. Some of them were from
important people. Henry was a little disappointed. She didn't
come right out and tell me, but I sensed it.

"Look, Henry," I explained. "I'm a plain and simple guy.
I don't belong in this social whirl. Exposition Park is my level
—that's where my friends are. I've come here for one purpose—to keep my title and get a professional contract. Nothing's going to interfere."

"Nothing will," Henry said.

And nothing did.

Frank Shields, who had given me much encouragement
during my visit to Forest Hills in 1948, again was in my
corner. That made me feel better. Frank, who had been the
nation's top-ranked player in 1933, is a sound tactician. He's
also a big handsome guy who knows how to wear clothes and
is poised and at ease in any kind of company. His polish and
mastery of the social graces interested me as much as his tennis tips, and I watched him carefully and tried to acquire
some of his self-assurance. I learned a lot from Frank, but to

this day I still don't know how to shake a lady's hand properly. I know enough to wait until she extends it—this puts all
the risk on her side. More often than not, I'll grip it like my
racket and the smile on fair lady's face suddenly becomes a
grimace.

After practice one day, Frank drove Henry and me to
the private home which was our headquarters during our
stay at Forest Hills. Along the way, Frank engaged in the
small talk that made him such a pleasant guy to have around.

"Did you ever think how lonely a game tennis is?" he suddenly asked.

"Lonely?" I countered. "With all those people around?"

He nodded. "Oh, they're around, of course, but they're not
on the court with you. You stand on a plot of finely manicured
grass, seventy-eight by twenty-seven feet. It's yours to defend. Any ball that comes into it must be hit back. It's like
having your country bombarded by the enemy. Only no
allies. You do it alone."

"Seventy-eight by twenty-seven," I mused. "Well, what do
you know!"

"You mean," Shields said in surprise, "you didn't know
the dimensions of a tennis court?"

"Never gave it a thought," I replied. "As long as *my* two
feet can cover all those feet, I figure I'm alright."

"I'll bet Ted Schroeder knows the dimensions," Frank
said casually, trying to needle me at the same time.

"Probably. Ted's a smart boy."

There was silence for a moment.

"I'll tell you one thing, though, Frank," I broke in. "Ted
will have to know more than just the size of the court if he's
going to get this title away from me this week."

"Atta boy!" Frank roared.

As the tournament got under way, the big crowds watched
our matches carefully. The early rounds were uneventful. I

got past Jack Geller, Straight Clark, and Jimmy Brink without losing a set. Schroeder kept pace by also winning every set in his first three matches. In the quarter-final round, however, I ran into my old left-handed nemesis, Art Larsen, and I had a battle on my hands. Carelessness on my part, plus some sensational hitting by Art in the fourth set, pushed this match to the limit. But by the fifth set my game was working well and there was no danger thereafter.

The semi-final round was much easier. My opponent, Frankie Parker, started off with a rush. He played almost perfect tennis to win the first set, and was within two points of grabbing the next set, before my big serve pulled me out of trouble. I wound up with eleven service aces in that set, winning it at 9-7. I knew I had Frankie now. The next two sets were mine and I was in the final round.

Schroeder had two stiff five-setters before he qualified for the finals. Frank Sedgman had Ted in trouble in the quarter-finals, before Schroeder rallied strongly to settle the issue in the fifth set. In the semi-finals, Billy Talbert, who had polished off Jaroslav Drobny in straight sets the previous day, jumped off to a 2-1 lead in sets at the intermission. But, once again, Ted came charging back, captured the fourth and fifth sets and landed in the final.

The setting for the final round resembled the corn-ballish plot of a grade-B Hollywood movie. Considering the perilous path any player has through a national championship tournament, it did seem somewhat miraculous that out of 101 players in the competition the two players perfectly cast for the drama of the final round should arrive for the rendezvous unscathed. Such things only happen in the movies. Nevertheless, there we were for our showdown, and America's tennis fans licked their chops in anticipation of the fireworks to come.

On the eve of the final, Shields invited Henry and me to dinner.

"Let's relax over a nice, thick steak," he suggested.

I declined with thanks, telling Frank we were going to a movie.

"Well, be sure to pick out something soothing," he advised.

I nodded.

Henry and I went to a double-horror show. But I slept like a baby that night.

The next morning, neither Henry nor I mentioned tennis. When we went to the West Side Tennis Club, there was no big scene at parting time—no emotion. Henry simply patted my hand lightly, turned and went off. There was no need for words—we knew what was in each other's heart.

In I went to the locker room, and, remembering my past pre-match experiences with Schroeder, I made a point of steering clear of him. I put on my tennis togs slowly. I felt good. Imagine that! Feeling good when you're about to play the most important match of your life against a guy who had beaten you seven times out of eight!

I examined my rackets carefully and an official came along.

"They're ready for you over there, Pancho," he said.

It was post-time.

During the warm up on the center court, Schroeder seemed as nonchalant as ever, but when the match got under way he became dead serious and aggressive. The early games indicated the tenseness of our play. Most points were won on errors, rather than placements. For thirty-two games it was serve and volley, serve and volley, and the capacity crowd of thirteen thousand howled in delight as it watched history in the making. The break came in the thirty-third game. Trailing, love-40 on my own serve, I stormed back to send the score to deuce. Schroeder took the advantage on a net cord shot. Now I went in for a volley and I hit the ball down the line, out of Ted's reach. Chalk dust flew in all directions as the ball hit the line. To my complete amazement, the linesman signaled, "Out."

That gave Ted the service break he needed, and when he held his own serve in the next game, he had the set, 18-16.

Tennis historians point to this set as one of the all-time best. Certainly it was one of the longest. But after struggling for an hour and thirteen minutes, I had nothing to show for my labor but a one set deficit. In a much shorter time, Schroeder had the second set, too.

At the start of the second set, Ted asked the umpire for permission to don spiked shoes. The grass was damp and slippery. The request was granted. It was a smart move—especially since I didn't own a pair of spikes and couldn't borrow any.

A lot of things started running through my mind now. That bad line call that cost me the first set still stuck in my craw. The spikes. It was shaping up as a bad day—a typical Schroeder-Gonzales match, I thought, where everything goes wrong for Pancho. Poor Pancho!

While I was feeling sorry for myself, Ted was piling up the points and he took the second set at 6-2.

Now the odds really were stacked against me. No one ever spotted Ted Schroeder the first two sets and lived to pull the match out of the fire. No sir, you just didn't get away with such things against this great clutch player. I had no argument to offer. And when the second set was over, my morale was cracked. My only thought now was to give the packed gallery a good match for their money—to play as hard as I could, even though my cause was almost hopeless.

With this aim, I ran through the first four games of the

third set rather easily. Ted then appeared to make a decision to let this set go and concentrate on finishing me off in the fourth set, after the intermission. I won the set, 6-1.

I showered and changed clothes during the intermission. Frank Shields came in.

"That first set was a tough one to lose," he consoled.

I nodded. "But it might be tougher on Ted in the fifth set," I told him.

"That's the spirit," Frank said, like a cheer-leader. "There's plenty of time to get him."

"How's Henry taking it?" I asked.

"Oh, she's been crying a little, but she's alright."

Frank now mapped out some strategy that was to play an important part in the rest of the match. He noted that Ted, when he was a point ahead, was using his second serve first and winning points on my weak return. I was standing too deep for this serve, expecting, of course, the big first serve. Frank told me to keep an eye on the marquee, where he was sitting. He would give me the signal when to move in for the softer serve. By being better prepared for this, I could move in behind my return of service and be ready to volley at the net.

Frank, sitting in the front row of the marquee seats, dangled his arms over the railing to signal to me. It paid big dividends.

In the fourth set, my serve was my best friend. This, combined with the fact that I was now handling Schroeder's service better, caused my spirits to soar. I moved out to 3-1, then to 5-2. At this point, a leather-lunged guy in the gallery, obviously referring to Schroeder's work as a refrigeration salesman, roared:

"Come on, Pancho, put Ted back in the deep freezer."

The gallery laughed, and suddenly I felt I had thirteen thousand people pulling for *me*. Pulling for Pancho—the "cheese champion." I took the set at 6-2, and we were all even. The fateful fifth set was at hand.

What would the betting odds be on such a fifth set? I don't know. Only four times in six decades of National championship play had a player dropped the first two sets and returned to win the match. But, of course, none of these was accomplished with Ted Schroeder as the opponent. Ted, a determined, gutty guy, was murder in that fifth set. He was such a consistent winner in five-set matches, that tennis addicts had altered the sports axiom to read: Never bet against Notre Dame, the New York Yankees, or Ted Schroeder in the fifth set."

But, frankly, I didn't think of odds or of Ted's reputation as the showdown started. I was strong. I was hitting good. And I was confident. A pretty good combination for any fellow to have in the crucial moments of play.

The games followed service through the first eight. In the ninth game, I cracked through Ted and all I had to do now was hold my own serve and the title was mine. Ted drove my first serve into the net, but I followed with a double fault and a netted backhand and I trailed, 15-30. Schroeder put the next delivery in the net and it was 30-all. Now I was two points away, but the crowd groaned as I went after a ball that would have gone "out" and clobbered it wildly. It was 30-40. Ted drove beyond the baseline for deuce and I quickly took the advantage by banging home a good placement. I stood at "match point."

The crowd sat in tomb-like silence. I looked across the net and saw my arch foe squirming and gritting his teeth. I kissed my racket and served. Ted returned. I fired it back and Ted took it on his forehand. The ball zoomed down the sideline, out of my reach. My heart must have stopped beating for the split second it took for the ball to land and the linesman to call his decision.

"Out," was the welcome call.

I was home. Winner and still champion.

I'll remember a lot of things about that moment. The generous tribute from the gallery; the look of astonishment on Ted's face; the genuine smiles and affection from so many of those who had been so certain I wouldn't win. But the picture of that wonderful moment that will stay with me always, is the photograph used by *American Lawn Tennis* on its cover. It showed Henry hugging me and smiling the most wonderful smile I've ever seen. And the caption read:

"The Last Laugh."

How true! How true!

7 The Years Slip By

Hardly had I returned from winning at Forest Hills when the telephone rang in my Los Angeles apartment and Henry announced, "Bobby Riggs."

In two giant strides I crossed the room and grabbed the phone. I had a pretty good idea of the nature of the call. Riggs rarely telephones anybody to pass the time of day in idle gossip.

"Hello, Bobby," I greeted, trying to control the excitement I felt.

"What's on for tonight, Pancho?" he asked.

"Not a thing," I answered, concealing the fact I had a bowling date.

He said, "Pick you up at eight, sharp. Something I want to talk over with you."

"Okay," I said. "I'll be ready."

He appeared on the stroke of eight, brief case in hand. From it he extracted some typewritten papers. Getting right to the point, he said, "I've got a contract for you to play Jack Kramer. A tour of the country. We'll go find a notary, sign, and wind it up."

I held up my hand like a traffic cop. "Not so fast, Bobby."

A faint trace of surprise crossed his face. "You want to tour with Jack, don't you? What's the problem?"

"Let's take it to Neil McCarthy," I proposed. "He's my adviser. If he says, 'Sign it,' I will."

McCarthy was a smart lawyer and he took a fatherly interest in me. He lived alone in a big house off Sunset Boulevard with a flock of servants to take care of him. Since he had lived in Arizona for a time, Neil numbered among his acquaintances many Mexicans and knew their special problems.

When, as an amateur, I was preparing to go to Wimbledon, he handed me four hundred dollars.

"Who do you want murdered?" I asked him.

He laughed.

"Take this money and buy yourself some clothes," he ordered. "You don't want the English to outdress you."

I thanked him, and when I left, he called after me, "Be sure to wear a necktie for a change."

After introducing Neil to Bobby we sat down while he read the contract. When he finished, his face was expressionless. With a slightly apologetic shrug of the shoulder he tore the contract into little pieces, dropping them to the floor.

"Come back tomorrow night and I'll show you a new contract," he said to Bobby.

The next night we were back and I signed. Bobby signed. The tour called for approximately 123 matches between Jack and myself; Kramer, World's Professional Champion vs. Gonzales the challenger. Jack was the King of the Courts— rated by many experts as one of the greatest players ever to reach this enviable position. Fresh from the amateur ranks, I was determined to snatch the crown from his head, and I was just cocky enough to think that I could do it.

I had a lot to learn.

We were in business together—Bobby, Jack, and I— partners in a great sports venture involving thousands of miles of travel over every conceivable type of roadbed constructed by highway engineers of mixed abilities. Roads are important on a tour. All traveling is done by car.

So closely did the agreement bind us together that it reminded me of a marriage contract with its "for better or for worse" clause. At least it did in substance.

I got the "worse."

I don't mean that the contract contained fine print or hidden or twisted interpretations. What I mean is I got the trouncing of my young life. Jack was merciless. He never relaxed. His "off" nights were few and far between. If I managed to dump him in Boston and foolishly start thinking I'd solved his all-court game, he'd thump me so terribly the next night in Providence I'd wonder if the strings in my racket weren't just ornamental.

Consequently, Jack wasn't doing the gate any good. How many persons, at the height of Rocky Marciano's career, would pay to see him fight a flyweight? Our tour wasn't much different. I was clearly overmatched, and it began to dawn on me that my game, at the age of twenty-one and less than a full year out of the amateurs, was a far cry from the peak of professionalism.

Prior to taking the court one night in Chicago, I overheard Jack talking to a well-wisher who was assuming the role of adviser.

"Better take it easy, Jack," the man said.

Glancing up from examining the strings of a racket, Jack inquired, "I don't understand."

"Well," the man went on, "I mean get smart."

"Smart?"

"Yeah. Toss Pancho a few matches. Keep the match score closer. You'll draw bigger crowds."

Slowly Jack straightened up. He was clutching the racket and I noticed his hand trembled, but his voice was steady as he replied, "The only thing I'll toss on this tour is you, if you don't get out of here."

The man took off like a rocket.

"Jack," I said, walking toward him, "I heard what you said."

He looked at me. His lower lip was shaking with rage. "Got any opinion on the subject?"

"You did the right thing," I said.

He calmed slightly. "I'm glad you agree," he said. "Now let me tell you something. I don't care if we lose money every night. I'll never let down one single point against you or anybody else on any tour. The public pays their money and they're going to see me at my best. And you too."

"You'll get no argument from me on that," I agreed.

Scooping up the rest of his rackets, Jack said, "Let's go."

I followed. He was still boiling mad when we were introduced to the crowd. We warmed up and began to play. I was a feather caught in a tornado as Jack exploded all his pent-up anger on the innocent white balls. At the end of the two sets, I had won only four games.

Jack walloped me ninety-six matches to twenty-seven on the tour, and I returned to Los Angeles dragging my tail behind me. For days I went around the house sullen, uncommunicative. Defeat burns me up and I was really afire. My attitude was hard on Henry.

"Richard," she said, "do I in any manner, shape, or form resemble Jack Kramer?"

I scowled, which was as close to a laugh as I could manage in the midst of my doldrums. My eyes roved her figure. "Not with those legs," I assured her.

"Then concentrate on my legs," she ordered, "and realize I'm not Jack Kramer. I'm your wife. I'm the girl you married. Remember? Don't take your Kramer losses out on me."

"I remember."

"Start treating me like your wife again and quit brooding," she commanded, and went on: "So you were beaten. He's the only man in the world who can do it."

"He'll never do it again," I vowed.

"Okay," she said, "but don't lose sight of the fact you gained plenty from the tour."

"Sure I did. I learned that when he comes to the net and I dump a soft one at his feet he . . ."

"No. Something else."

"What?"

"You gained seventy-five thousand dollars, more money than we dreamed existed. Let's do something with the money. Something wise."

We talked it over and late that night decided we would buy a modest house and also one for my mom and dad. From now on money wasn't going to be one of our worries, if we had any worries. Maybe it didn't grow on trees as the saying goes, but it grew on tennis courts, and if I made seventy-five thousand dollars my first year as a pro, what would I make my second and my third?

This was the thinking of an inexperienced mind. The thinking of a drunken sailor on payday.

Almost immediately the shadows dimmed the glitter of the gold. In 1951, my second year as a pro, I worked long hours but played little tennis. It was profitable for those calloused gentlemen who figure percentages however, and run legalized luxury poker parlors close to Los Angeles and have habitual customers like Richard Alonzo Gonzales. Slowly, yet always surely, they relieve you of your chips. Some nights you win, some nights you lose, but in the long run after hours of sitting, the money fritters away. And I sadly discovered it went a lot faster than I'd been able to earn it on the courts.

The card players I pitted wits against were the type that could sit calmly for an hour, staying out of pots, waiting for cinches. I couldn't. I can't play this way. I push my hands too strongly. I bluff. And I get caught.

Why was I squandering away the nights gambling? The motive was obvious. No tennis matches were lined up for me. I had become an also-ran. I needed the tonic of action. Gambling filled the vacuum, although it lacked the real thrill of tennis.

I've lost as much as one thousand dollars in one night at cards, and more than two thousand dollars in a session at the dice tables in Las Vegas. I like to forget the bad nights, but as most fellows do who have a thirst for competition, I remember the good ones. It's the same way in tennis. The details of a bad day often are vague, but you always remember everything about your big wins—even the temperature, the color of your opponent's eyes, and what you ate for breakfast. My big match at the card table came in a game of Stud Low Ball, table stakes. I won $890 for the hand, holding a seven-five low.

All the while I was hounding Bobby Riggs. Finally he made clear the facts of life. They were both enlightening and discouraging.

"Pancho," he said, "you're dead as a drawing card."

"Dead!" I repeated.

"Professional tennis is a funny sport," Bobby explained. "All the public really cares about is the champ and the challenger. Mainly the challenger. The stamp of amateurism hasn't fully dried on him yet, so he's a knight in shining armor, the people's choice, a fresh new personality.

"Like I was?"

"Like you were," he agreed, continuing: "You're past tense now. Your name's worth nothing. You came, you saw—and Jack Kramer conquered.

"I see," I said sourly.

Bobby's next words failed to lift the gloom. "Perhaps some day," he said, "we can build you up again."

"And in the meantime?"

"Keep playing, keep in condition, keep your weight down, save your money, and stand by."

His words were hard to swallow and bitter to the taste. My future suddenly darkened. True, there would be a few exhibitions, a few lessons and a few sporadic tournaments. Not enough competition. When you've got a body that continually cries for action, you've got to heed the cries.

Following my card-playing disaster I was approached by Arzy Kunz who, at the time, operated the Olympic Tennis Shop at Exposition Park. Frank Poulain had retired from tennis and Arzy rented from him.

Arzy came right to the point. He doesn't enjoy talking any more than I do. A guy we both knew once cracked, "If Arzy and you had a two-man debate, you'd just sit facing each other across a table in utter silence. At the end of the allotted time one or the other would say, 'Let's go out and have a beer.' End of debate."

So Arzy said to me, "Want to buy my tennis shop? I'm thinking of moving out on LaCienega." The location was near some fine public courts in Beverly Hills.

"What've you got to sell and how much?" I asked him.

"A little equipment and a lot of good will," he returned, mentioning a price.

I went over to the shop with him. Twenty minutes later

he handed me the key. I now owned the shop which I had loved as a kid—the place which once had been my refuge from truant officers.

I started stringing rackets and selling balls, but I'd knock off work if somebody like Oscar Johnson came by looking for a game. Later Oscar became the National Tennis Association Champion (Negro Championship). I tried to coach him a little. It wasn't easy. I'd never had any tutoring myself.

Often I'd play social tennis on other courts—sometimes at Griffith Park, where, after a workout, I'd talk a little tennis in Fred Moll's shop. Fred had a good business and sold more rackets in a day than I sold all week.

At night I'd play basketball in a semi-pro league, or bowl. Ten blocks from my home is the Twentieth Century Recreation Bowl run by Charley Peroni, a high-average roller and teacher. Charley, together with the other boys who hang out there, knows nothing about tennis and cares less. This was evidenced by what Charley said to Al Stump, a magazine writer who was doing a story on me called, "All Dressed Up and No Place to Play."

"This Gonzales!" Peroni told Stump, "I don't know anything about his other game, but he could be another Andy Varipapa at bowling if he worked at it. I've seen him bowl at least 75 games of 240 pins or more. Some of the sharpest shooters in town hang out here and this Gonzales cleans 'em out in pot games . . . He's got that great wrist action."

Three nights each week I'd roll with my wife in a Recreation League. It gave me something to do, helped me work off steam. I enjoy the sounds in a bowling alley. A man can create his own thunder. They tell me that in Greek Mythology there was some guy named Zeus, who hurled thunderbolts. When I throw a strike, if old Zeus can hear me he must think he's back in business.

My day would start pretty early in the morning. Don't take

my word for it—ask the neighbors. None of them needed alarm clocks. Late sleeping was impossible, for they'd be awakened by the sounds of my hitting tennis balls off the back wall of my garage. This is good practice. I can beat any player in the world today but not that old Devil wall. No matter how you hit the ball—hard or soft—the wall always returns it.

After a workout with the wall, I'd go down to the shop. What I dreaded most was opening the mail and encountering business forms that needed attention. I hate paperwork. I didn't even like adding up the receipts, but this wasn't a big problem. There wasn't too much to add up usually. A small business can be a headache to a man without a business head, and believe me, my business was small.

To be sure, I had many tempting offers to teach a few rich people in Hollywood and Beverly Hills for fees much fatter than the prevailing Southern California hourly rates. It would involve taking a paunchy man in his mid-fifties, who should be wearing a corset, and showing him how to swing a racket so that he wouldn't look like a fat lady chopping wood. Southern California has plenty of self-styled pros who would jump at the chance to teach such pupils. These fellows have no club affiliations, doing most of their teaching on private courts.

I passed up most of these opportunities, although in a weak moment I did agree to teach a female movie star. She had everything—looks, figure, big home, private tennis court. Fifty bucks per lesson was the price, and if it involves just straight tennis, that's awfully good money. A lesson never runs much over an hour.

A servant showed me to the court and informed that the mistress would be along in a minute. I had a large straw basket filled with practice balls which I set down at the rear of the court and waited. Then I saw her approaching. What a walk! It belonged on a runway—not a tennis court, but I wasn't complaining.

Introductions over, I showed her the proper grip, made clear the rudiments of the swing, sent her deep into the court and began feeding her easy balls. She fanned the air hopelessly, handling the racket as if it were a giant fly swatter. Occasionally she made feeble contact on the wood. She was setting the game back about twenty years, but her classic figure made this something less than revolting.

Walking around the net I advised, "Just relax and let me swing for you." I stood behind her maneuvering her arm through the correct motions. Slowly she leaned back until her head rested against my chest. The racket grew limp in her hand. Her eyes were misty. It was a throwback to some corny movie scene of another era.

"Oh, Pancho," she whispered, and her eyelashes actually fluttered.

"You interested in taking a lesson?" I asked curtly.

"A lesson? What *kind* of a lesson?" she panted.

I tried to ignore the obvious come-on.

"Well, I'm supposed to teach you *tennis,*" I replied, trying to stick to business.

"Oh yes, *tennis!*" she laughed. "And I'm supposed to relax! Then let's try relaxing back at the house."

Fingering the collar of my shirt she fluttered her eyelashes some more. I squirmed mentally. "Look, Beautiful," I said bluntly, "I'm married, and . . ."

"So am I," was the prompt reply. "That makes us even."

"Not quite."

"What can your wife do that I can't do?" she wanted to know.

"Well, she can *bowl* for one thing," I laughed.

"Anything else?"

"She can cook beans the way I like 'em."

She tossed in the sponge now, and with one brief, but noisy, salvo, told me to take my tennis lesson elsewhere.

Now I don't want anyone to think I'm boasting of my virtues. The story simply points up how seriously I take my tennis.

As I was pouring over the books in my shop one breezy day and hoping the wind might blow through the doorway and carry away the tantalizing paperwork, the telephone rang. It was Mom and she wanted me to come over.

"Anything wrong?" I questioned. Mom rarely called me during the day.

"It's about Sonny," was all she would say.

I wondered what had happened to my brother, Ralph. Mom briefed me. Ralph—called Sonny by our family—was at the hard-to-handle age. He owned a beat-up 1934 Ford coupe and would hop into it right after dinner and take off for a pool parlor. This hangout, Mom felt, was full of characters that might shape Ralph's own character the wrong way.

When I got to the house I tried to suppress a grin and failed.

"You think this is a joke?" Mom demanded.

"No," I assured her. "I was just thinking it wasn't too many years ago that I was considered the bad boy of the family."

Mom shrugged off the past. "You are the oldest," she stated. "He'll listen to you."

I put my arm around her shoulder. "Don't worry, I'll take care of it."

I located the pool hall, and Ralph was there as usual. His jaw dropped when he saw me.

"Shoot a game, Dick?" he invited.

I presented a proposition. "Shoot you for your car. Double a fair price or nothing."

"You're too good."

"Okay then, follow me over to my shop," I said. "I want to talk to you."

On the way out I collared the owner of the place and said, "This boy's under age. If I catch him in here again I'll see that you're reported."

When we reached the shop, I asked Ralph for the keys to his car. Puzzled, he handed them over. "I'll be keeping these," I said, mentioning he was too young to own an automobile.

He protested. "I've got a big investment tied up in this car. You can't just move in and take over."

"That isn't exactly what I'm doing. I'm buying out your interest."

He didn't answer.

"And don't jack up the price," I warned.

We settled on fifty dollars. I put the car in a bus parking lot near my shop, where it sat for two weeks gathering rust.

In the middle of a slow business day I decided to look it over. I threw up the hood and started thinking and dreaming.

That dream was to cost me seventy-five hundred dollars!

Beneath that battered, old hood I installed a 1951, eight-cylinder Cadillac engine "goosed-up" to 375 horsepower. Wide open, she could hit 160 miles per hour on a straightaway. No reasonable facsimile now existed between Ralph's former car and what I had now. It was renovated into a low slung, white-painted, stripped-down, sleek hunk of metal. I'd gone "hotrod happy."

Contrary to the opinion of many who have fixed ideas, the average hotrod driver is not a juvenile delinquent or a case of arrested mentality. He works hard on his car—and working keeps a boy out of trouble. He doesn't necessarily roar around corners on two wheels, or try to outspeed police cars. He is, for the most part, a sane, sensible driver—perhaps a little noisier than the average stock car operator. He races at one of several places. The king spot around here—the Indianapolis of the hotrodders—is an asphalt strip at Saugus, California. All races are under official supervision.

Saugus, forty miles north of Los Angeles, the capital of jalopy racing, has a lightning fast "drag-strip." Here, I wear coveralls, a crash helmet and drive like hell. It's a far cry from the sedate atmosphere of Forest Hills.

Hotrod racing *can* be dangerous. Safety is purely up to the individual. I'll admit its pitfalls to anyone but Henry. You start from a standstill. The getaway is important. You zoom down the converted airfield runway toward the finish line, a quarter of a mile away. I can reach a speed of around 70 mph in 500 feet.

Sure there's risk. If everything isn't in perfect mechanical shape you may blow higher than a kite. If you're unlucky you may get a broken arm, busted leg, or even worse. Sure, death might be breathing down your neck but that doesn't mean it has to catch up with you.

What's the reward? It can't be measured materially. The prize trophy is worth about three dollars. I suppose it's the feeling of excitement, the emotional release, that satisfies.

Henry put up strong arguments in the beginning. She was fighting a losing cause. The word-battle ran like this:

"Think of me, Pancho."

"I do."

"Think of your family."

"I do."

"Can't you give it up?"

"Sure—but I don't want to."

"Want me to be a young widow?"

"No—but you look good in black."

"You're hopeless."

"And you're beautiful."

And that's the way it went.

Another sport I tried was golf. Frank Parker and Bobby Riggs introduced me to the fairways, and considering the way I dug them up the first time it wasn't a pleasant meeting. After three weeks, however, I carded a 75. Several friends urged me to switch from tennis to the links. The great tennis ace, Ellsworth Vines, had made a profitable change.

"No," I argued, "my heart will always be in tennis."

Anyway, golf was a trifle too slow for me. I loved smacking the ball; liked to watch it soar through the air. What bothered me was the lull between shots. There's nothing to do but walk. That's a little too mild for me.

Because of the expiration of my contract with Bobby Riggs and no renewal in sight, I signed with sports promoter Jack Harris. Harris, who had promoted several tennis tours in the past, was trying to crack the Riggs-Kramer stranglehold on the pro shows.

This was okay with me. Personally, I didn't care who was the boss just as long as I could return to the courts. So from 1952 through 1953, I belonged to Jack Harris. I stagnated.

Another activity I developed to take up the slack was breeding dogs. Boxers. I accomplished this by the air of patience, nature, and a wired-in dog run in the back yard. I'm glad no neighborhood popularity contests were held. With the barking of dogs and the slapping sounds of tennis balls bouncing off the garage wall, undoubtedly I would have finished last.

Henry and I sold some of the pups for prices ranging from $75 to $125. But we didn't make much money; not even after Duchess, a fine female had delivered her third litter. Although boxers aren't supposed to be hunting or retrieving dogs, one of the pups disproved the theory by bringing in several missing tennis balls every evening. Today, the dogs have taken over the house. Friends who keep getting a constant busy signal when telephoning us have often reported the instrument out of order. It isn't true. The pups keep knocking the receiver off the hook.

During these years of tennis oblivion I had no club affiliations, although any time I wanted to play at the Los Angeles Tennis Club—the Forest Hills of the West Coast—George Tolley, one of its pros, arranged a game for me. Of course I enjoy playing anybody, but I needed competition tougher than the club players could offer if I wanted to elevate my game to the Jack Kramer level. Patting the ball socially wasn't going to advance my game very far.

Periodically the local tennis set invited me to cocktail parties. At this juncture, let me sound off loud and clear on what my opinion is of these so-called revelries. I may have been the toast of the tennis clique after the second straight year I won the national championships, but at a cocktail party I was like an olive that found its way into a glass of bourbon instead of a martini. In short, I was a misfit.

Frankly, cocktail parties bore me silly. A lot of people, all dressed up, drink too much and try to outshout each other, claiming to be what they aren't. I can't be something I'm not because I am what I want to be—at all times. If that doesn't make sense, skip it. Besides, I don't care about alcohol. I can take it in moderation or leave it alone. Generally, I leave it alone. I recognize it as a condition destroyer.

I like to circulate. It's hard for me to stand or sit in one place very long. You can't move around very much at a cocktail gathering hemmed in by a solid phalanx of bodies; there's always the fear of spilling your drink on some woman's expensive dress.

And speaking of women at these groups, they'll back you into a corner and either tell you their life story or want to know yours. Some of them have asked to feel my arm muscles. One felt my calves. "I'm just taking a muscular survey," this

one said. Muscles seem to interest women. Maybe it's because if a girl snares a guy with a bunch of them, she figures
she'll have no trouble getting him to move the furniture
around every time she goes into a redecoration mood.

Now I wouldn't mind a cocktail party so much if when I
came in I'd be handed a printed floor plan with all exits
clearly marked. Then I'd be able to slip away unnoticed at
the appropriate time. Even that wouldn't be easy when you
find yourself pinned against a wall by a bunch of chattering
females.

Getting back to tennis, the dead-stop in my career ended
temporarily, late in 1953, when Jack Kramer called me. Besides being one of the foremost tennis players in the con-
troversial history of the game, Jack has something else in his
favor. He's an astute businessman. This is a rare combination, and I've always regretted not having such dual talents.

Jack had taken over the promotional reins of pro tennis
from Bobby Riggs and his new organization was known as
World Tennis, Inc. Jack listed himself as general manager.
Olin Parks, a former sporting goods representative was tour
director, and Myron McNamara, an excellent public courts
player was the publicity director.

Jack invited me to his office. I sat uncomfortably, in a hard
chair. No soft seats were available. I suspect that Jack arranged it so, purposely, with the object of denying a prospect
any form of comfort. Jack, therefore, gained the advantage.
The prospect couldn't relax, doze or let his thoughts stray.
He had to pay close attention to anything Jack might be selling. And Jack usually was selling.

Jack had crushed Frank Sedgman, the Aussie ace, on a
national tour in 1953, and now was in virtual retirement,
appearing infrequently in doubles play or a fill-in match. I
had gradually developed mastery over him. He was past his
prime. Age and an arthritic back condition were taking a

heavy toll. In our rivalries since my lambastings on the tour, I held an 11-5 edge. My game was steadily ascending. I had blown the U. S. National Professional Championship to Segura in 1952, but took the title the next year by beating Don Budge. Ground strokes had always been my weakness. Now, if necessary, I could stay in the back court and outstroke the best of them.

I studied Jack as he launched into his proposals. He wanted me for a round-robin tour against Sedgman, the crowd-pleasing Segura, and the old redhead, Budge. The standings of the wins and losses would be tabulated, and the lion's share would go to the victor. I was ready to roar like a lion.

Bouncing around on the balls of his feet—the same bounce he does when he begins his service—Jack was waving a contract in the air and talking about the advantages contained therein. When Jack talks he projects and his listeners are both charmed and hypnotized. The only challenge he's ever had in this personality projection business comes from Nancy Chaffee Kiner, now semi-retired from serious tournament competition. Nancy's personality reaches even those in the fringe area and on days when her shorts are too tight she doesn't even have to talk.

Anyway, Jack was reaching me. Every time he mentioned money, the entire room seemed to take on a golden hue. You see, from 1951 to 1954 I had lost most of my contact with income, and this money-talk was like meeting up with a long-lost friend.

In the middle of a long sentence, which included more words than generally come out of me during an entire hour, I caught Jack at a comma and said loudly, "Just a second, Jake!"

Contract trailing from his hand, he walked over close and said, "What is it, Pancho?"

"There's only one thing that keeps me from signing your contract."

His eyes narrowed, pupils contracting. I could tell he was thinking of money. "And what might that be, Pancho?" he asked pleasantly.

"I haven't got a pen," I told him.

He stared at me incredulously for a long moment, regained his composure and whipped out a fountain pen. It wasn't one of those ball point jobs, but something in the fifteen dollar class. You can tell a successful promoter by his fountain pen.

"Here," he said, handing me the pen and smoothing the contract on the desk surface. "Write your full name and no Pancho, please."

I signed Richard Alonzo Gonzales.

Maybe I was on the road back.

The only business matter on hand was disposal of the Exposition Park Tennis Shop. Frank Poulain still owned the property along with an adjoining restaurant. Elsie Gabel, a former San Francisco tournament player who did a good stringing job, moved in.

I won the round robin, but it wasn't exactly a howling financial success. However, it proved I could beat anyone in the world. The year I clashed with Kramer to initiate our tour in Madison Square Garden, eighteen thousand tennis fanatics showed up. I earned $5,400 for a single night's play. The round robin drew only 4,300 paying fans. In smaller places hardly more than four to five hundred turned out.

At the conclusion of this tour, I went to tennis-booming Australia. Playing with the pair of local heroes—Sedgman and McGregor—plus Segura, we packed them in. Attendance records were smashed in Perth, Adelaide, White City, Newcastle, Melbourne. I was at the peak of my game, inspired by a guarantee plus an individual prize of one thousand pounds ($2,800) for each tournament won. I swept the tour, beating

Sedgman, 16 matches to 9, McGregor, 15-0, and Segura, 4-2.
I killed them in Australia.

From Australia we moved northward to Tokyo and then
backtracked to Manila. The crowds were fantastic. The press
gave us page one billings and four-column photos. More than
fifteen thousand fans stood in line for hours on our final stop
in Seoul, Korea. We created much goodwill.

Yes, dollar-wise, 1954 was a profitable year. It was good to
be back in action again, on top, swatting the ball all over the
world, playing before enthusiastic crowds.

I came home feeling like a million dollars. The feeling
didn't last long. Not one reporter was on hand at Los Angeles
International Airport. If newspaper readers donned strong
glasses and meticulously read local sports pages they might
have found a brief notice at the bottom of a column:

> "Richard (Pancho) Gonzales returned to Los Angeles today
> after completing a professional tennis tour in which he
> traveled many thousands of miles. His future plans are un-
> certain."

Back to reality!

8 The Dead-End Street

Professional tennis is a unique sport. It has changed little since C. C. (Cash and Carry) Pyle came up with the play-for-pay notion some three decades ago. Pyle's headliners for that first pro tour were Suzanne Lenglen, the incomparable French star, and Vincent Richards, the so-called "Boy Wonder" of his day. Since that time, the greatest names in tennis have made the natural transition from amateur to professional, but the format for the pro game has remained the same. It has not developed its full potential—as has been the case with golf. And it still depends largely on the excitement stirred up in the amateur ranks for its *own* success.

If the amateurs produce an outstanding champion, or a colorful performer of top-notch ability, it almost always means the pros have a potential headliner for another national tour. But when the amateurs have a quiet year, the

114

pros suffer, too. Pro tennis audiences demand new faces, fresh challengers—the very best tennis produced by the world's best players.

In 1955, pro tennis turned down a dead-end street. I followed the same discouraging road. There was no pro tour. No national pro tournament. No future to speak of.

I had run out of competition. To be sure, there were plenty of competent players around the circuit, but no one who would attract cash customers on a pro junket. Other sports champions had suffered the same fate—Joe Louis, Bobby Jones, Willie Hoppe—to name a few. I had virtually sealed my doom by blasting Dinny Pails and Frank Parker, 45 matches to 7, in Australia.

"Why not go and live in Australia?" urged a friend. "They're tennis crazy over there."

I shook my head.

"How you gonna eat the rest of your life?"

I shrugged my shoulder.

In the meantime, I kept practicing. My game was never better. Two of the leading Italian players—Guiseppe Merlo and Fausto Gardini—were in this country for coaching. Eleanor Tennant, who tutored Maureen Connolly, was furnishing them with instruction. I saw them at the Los Angeles Tennis Club and invited them to have a game. They won a total of one game in four sets. And they'd been cutting quite a swath in European amateur circles.

Seeking out Kramer, I argued with him long and futilely. I insisted he find an opponent for me.

Jack shook his head. "I'd have to get a robot."

"What about Seixas or Trabert or Hoad or Rosewall?" I countered.

"Right now they can't beat Segura, let alone you. Maybe later."

"Can't *something* be done?"

He was pessimistic. "I haven't any solution," he said.
"Hoad and Rosewall seem about two years away. They're
only twenty, you know. It all adds up to one final conclusion,
Pancho."

"And that is?"

"You're too good."

Some predicament! Twenty-six years old, in the prime of
my tennis career, and no one to play. For obvious reasons I
followed the amateurs closely in 1955, noting that Tony
Trabert swept Wimbledon and the U. S. championships at
Forest Hills, only to run afoul of the Australian "Whiz Kids,"
Hoad and Rosewall, in Davis Cup play.

Kramer moved in immediately, signing Trabert to a pro
contract. And then he set his sights on Hoad and Rosewall.
Jack knew what he was doing. Trabert, the United States
and Wimbledon winner, could tour the country against the
powerful Aussies in a replay of the Davis Cup. It was box
office. On paper it couldn't miss, if he managed to sign Rosewall and Hoad. It was a big "if" too.

Where did Pancho Gonzales, who could beat anyone in
the world, fit into this picture? He didn't. He was left out in
the cold.

Meanwhile, the National Professional Hard Court Tennis
Championship was on tap at the fashionable Beverly Wilshire Hotel. This was staged by my good friend Frank Feltrop,
the hotel pro. From the moment I entered amateur competition Frank had always encouraged me and kept pounding it
into me that I could be the greatest.

Trabert was conspicuous by his absence from the Beverly
Hills tournament. A reporter asked me why, and I pulled no
punches in my answer.

"He couldn't win it, and it would take the edge off the coming Kramer tour."

Vincent X. Flaherty of the *Los Angeles Examiner* took up

the cudgel for me, writing: "Gonzales unquestionably is the greatest tennis player in the world today and, undoubtedly, is one of the greatest performers the game ever has had."

I'd never argue that point.

Flaherty then made what I thought was a classic comparison. He said: "Professional tennis is the only sport in which the Babe Ruth is left in the dugout while .220 hitters go to bat."

He also wrote something that I hoped Henry wouldn't read. "Meanwhile," Flaherty said, "Gonzales might take a shot at motion pictures. He has been approached on the idea. Certainly the movies haven't a more virile specimen of masculinity. He causes the feminine heartstrings to make like soft chimes. If you don't think so, take in the Beverly Wilshire tournament during the next few days and listen to the ladies of the audience make lady-like sounds of total enchantment while tall, dark, and handsome performs."

Henry didn't mention the article, and although we subscribe to Flaherty's newspaper and she often glances at the sports pages, I was pretty certain she hadn't seen it. Later that same evening she asked me quite seriously, "Pancho, have you ever sued anybody?"

"Certainly not," I said. "Why?"

She acted miffed, announcing, "I may."

"Now what's someone done to you?"

"Oh, not to me. Somebody said something about you."

"Slanderous?"

"No," she said. "Libelous."

"Really? In the newspaper? What was it?"

She said with a very straight face, "A man named Flaherty wrote that you are a virile specimen."

"And those are grounds for a suit?"

"Certainly," Henry said, her dark eyes soft, "unless you prove to me he was right."

"Right now?"

"This very second," she said, "and I quote, 'tall, dark, and handsome.' "

"I'll prove it," I said, pulling her toward me.

She never sued.

I won the tournament by downing Segura in the finals, 21-19, 6-3, 6-4. While the tourney was progressing Kramer was dickering with the two boys from Australia. It appeared a foregone conclusion to the press that they would sign. Kramer had strongly hinted that the deal was in the bag. But the bag had a hole in it. Both Hoad and Rosewall, undoubtedly acting on the urging of the Australian Lawn Tennis Association, turned down the flattering offer.

It was a blow to Kramer's plans, but now my chances brightened.

As a matter of fact, they were glowing when, together with my lawyer, Lou Warren, I met with Jack. To preserve some of the Australian flavor, Kramer had signed Rex Hartwig, the number three Aussie. Yet someone had to oppose Tony, and Hartwig wasn't good enough for that. It looked like I had stepped in through the back door. We conferred far into the night. Lou's gracious wife, Dorothy, kept pouring hot coffee and serving her specialty of the house, homemade almond cakes.

Lou's fifteen-year-old son, Earl, kept dogging my footsteps. He's tennis wild, and I had given him one of my old rackets. Twice Lou told the boy to go to bed, but when a youngster is sports-minded such an order is apt to fall on deaf ears.

"Oh, well," Lou finally said, giving up, "he might want to become a lawyer some day—Lord forbid—and he may get some pre-legal training out of this meeting.

Soon after the session opened it was evident Jack needed me. And I needed Jack. It was equitable thinking which, combined with wishful thinking, could be worked out thusly:

Kramer plus Gonzales vs. Trabert reduced to a common denominator means money.

"Tony and you should draw," Jack remarked. "He's the world's champ. It'll be a real pro vs. amateur test. I'll play Segura against Hartwig in the preliminary, and team you and Segura against them in the doubles."

I nodded. Lou nodded. Jack nodded. We had a deal. The next day I was signed, sealed and delivered.

While Lou and Jack were engaged in discussion, I was doing a lot of thinking. It seemed as if I had suddenly matured—that there was a transformation in my thinking processes, an awareness of duties to wife and family. If Tony beat me, I was through. Perhaps for good. On the other hand, if I beat Tony I would still be only twenty-seven years old, with a good three to five years, and possibly longer, left for me to stay on top. I had to. I was now the father of three boys.

I recalled overhearing an Eastern tennis bigwig describe me over a bridge table. My ears are pretty sensitive at long range—especially if someone's talking about me.

"Pancho Gonzales," said the brass hat, "is 25 per cent primeval animal, 25 per cent lazy and 50 per cent good sport."

I would alter this description. The animal part could stay, but the percentage of laziness was out. Sometimes in the past it had been hard for me to rise to a peak for each match. Things were going to be different. I'd fight in each match like it was the finals of an important tournament. The way Kramer blasted me, I'd try to blast Tony. It meant my future bread and butter.

At the conclusion of the meeting I casually mentioned to Jack, "I got sort of a feeler from a movie company. They might be interested in 'The Pancho Gonzales Story' if I beat Tony Trabert."

Jack cocked his head in my direction. "If there's a part open for a villain, recommend me, will you?"

I looked at him. His face was dead serious.

9 A Tour Isn't Just a Tour

The word "tour" has beautiful implications. One thinks of travel advertisements where the American, accompanied by a covy of suitcases plastered with enchanting labels, cruises leisurely about the more interesting portions of the world. Usually his neatly tailored pockets are stuffed with travelers checks, and if he has a single worry in the world, it's merely whether to skip the Balearic Islands in favor of more sunning time at Cannes.

"Tour" when applied to tennis is not even remotely related to such luxury. "Grind" is a better definition. Whereas the international tourist often returns a little on the obese side after lapping up foreign culinary creations, the tennis-tourer comes back lean, jaded, and with a stomach that needs refurbished lining.

The tennis tour tests a man's endurance, patience, and

courage. The day-to-day overland travel; the nightly tension of the "big match"; the need for being pleasant under the worst conditions combine to provide a set of conditions seldom encountered by any athlete in another sport. The greatest strain, however, seemed to be on my digestive tract. On these tours a man eats the lousiest food that ever failed to find a garbage can.

Before domestic chefs try to boil me in hot lard, let me clarify that I love American food. But I like to sit back and enjoy it. On the Trabert tour I ate in 102 different cities—also representing the number of matches I played against Tony. On this grind you might polish off a big dinner in Birmingham and not digest it until you have reached Memphis.

I had plenty of trepidation about the 1955 tour with Tony. Tony Trabert of Cincinnati, clean-cut and crew-cut tennis hopeful, began blossoming in 1953. Billy Talbert, one-time captain of the American Davis Cup Team, took him under his wing, teaching him tricks not found in instructional pamphlets. Tony won the U. S. Singles title, also scored at Wimbledon, cornered the French Singles title twice, and earned berths on the U. S. Davis Cup Team. He played a superb game and his typical all-American boy appearance made him a gallery favorite.

I discussed the impending Trabert tour with Henry. I'd always heard that no man is a hero to his valet. I have no valet, but I have a wife, and I guess she comes under that heading because she has to pick up the clothes I scatter around our home. I found I was wrong. I was a *hero* to her, and to let her down would be an awful blow to her pride.

"If I win the tour," I told her, "you get all the credit."

She swore softly. She never did this.

I raised an eyebrow and kept it raised when I heard her say, "Listen, Richard. I read a lot when you're away from

home. In most success stories I've noticed that the woman behind the man gets credit for pushing and prodding and
eventually making the man what he is. She inspires him. She
helps him. In my case it isn't true. I never helped push you
toward the top."

I insisted that she did.

Catching her breath, she went on: "No. You've got a motor
inside that does all that."

"You've always been a part of all this . . ."

"Sure, but a small part. I simply wind the motor up sometimes," she answered.

"Well, wind it tight," I said. "Wind it tight enough to last
for 102 matches."

Her dark head nodded. "I will. But," she warned, "don't
let it snap or it will knock your head off as well as mine and
the three boys."

I knew what she meant.

I looked at the Trabert tour as a reprieve. It was a chance
to come charging back to the lucrative big-time after once
having been sentenced to tennis oblivion. A chance to get on
top and stay on top. Oh, sure, I had won the National Professional Championship four times and had defeated all the
great players of the world, but that wasn't enough. If I lost to
Trabert, I was a bum again—unemployed, unwanted. If I
beat him, he was a bum. Someone had to come out of it a
bum. I didn't want it to be me.

I played for peanuts. My share for the toil and sweat was
fifteen thousand dollars, plus a percentage of the foreign gate.
The foreign gate was a short South American tour. Tony was
to receive a minimum of eighty thousand dollars. The players had to pay their own traveling expenses.

A little lop-sided? Yes, but these were the best arrangements my lawyer, Lou Warren, could wrangle out of Jack
Kramer, and if this little man with the big mind couldn't

do better, I was sure nobody else could. In other words, I was second money, and my thoughts on that matter were bitter.

"Why, Lou?" I said desperately. "Tell me *why?*"

Lou doesn't beat around bushes. His voice is soft and soothing. You have to lean forward in your chair to hear. Yet his words can explode in your brain. And they stick.

"I'll tell you why," he said. "You're on probation. Some people think you're unreliable. Immature. You've got a 'the-hell-with-everything' attitude."

Angry blood began burning around my temples. "I don't care what people think. I know that . . ."

Lou interrupted. "That's where you're wrong. What people think is of prime importance. They pay to see you. When they open a newspaper, they want to read that you're champion of the world. If the people know it, it helps in this business."

I thought it over and replied, "All I read about now is Jack Kramer. You'd think he was still on top. Why, the guy is thirty-four years old!"

"Sure," Lou agreed. "But his age doesn't matter with the public. He could be ninety-four, and they'd still think he could beat you."

"Why?"

"Why?" Because Jack has had wonderful press relations. He's left a lasting impression. The public won't begin to forget him for a long time. It might hurry their memory along, though, if, if . . ."

"If I beat Trabert?" I cut in, impatiently.

"That could do it," Lou replied.

I called on Jack Kramer at his World Tennis, Inc. office. I feel like a fish out of water in offices. They suffocate me. They're always cluttered with typewriters, files, and various machines to do jobs faster. Having tinkered with hotrods, I'm sure I could take any of these machines apart and put

them together again, but a simple procedure such as dictating
a letter to a girl sitting behind a desk would scare me half to
death.

Facing the man who made Bobby Riggs, Frank Sedgman
and me disappear from the headlines, I inquired, "Jake,
what's going to happen?"

Kramer chewed on a pencil, bounced to his feet and said,
"I'm not sure. You're a question mark. I don't know how the
public's going to react to you . . . if they take to you."

"You worried?" I asked.

"Why not?" he returned the question, stating, "I've got
money at stake."

"What have I got at stake?"

"Only a reputation that you haven't really established."

"Should I be worried?"

"Sure," he said, with a forced smile. "Aren't you?"

I nodded a weak affirmative.

"Go out and beat his ears off," were Jack's final words.

I was sure he'd said the same thing to Tony Trabert. It
was the old situation of the promoter encouraging his two
fighters to battle each other for the sake of the show.

For the first time in my life, responsibilities were weighing
heavily upon me. Carefree was a word that seemed associated with a distant past. I launched into a physical fitness
program, setting up my own training rules. This was the
least of my worries. The hot California sun beating down on
the concrete courts helped me melt off excess weight. I dieted,
too, although I didn't cut out the beans. That's something I
could never do. My game seemed on the upgrade. I was hitting sharp, and I felt mean. I worked on the two most important items in pro tennis—the volley and the serve. Conquer
them and you've got the game licked.

I began to feel hard around the stomach—a vital consideration. I've never seen an athlete with a roll of fat around the middle who was master over anything but a fork and spoon. When the tour reached New York a reporter queried, "How's your condition?" and when I said "Fine," he hauled off and punched me in the stomach. The blow was unexpected and stung, but I took it in stride.

"That's where it counts," he said. "You'll be alright."

Mental attitude also is important in training. To achieve this I went in for brain-washing, hammering one thought home—I can beat Tony Trabert. Under my system, I even built up a hatred for a man I'd met only a few times and who had always seemed pleasant.

When Tony reached Los Angeles, I watched him work out. I couldn't help but admire his game. He had everything —fine stroking, sound judgment, determination. Perhaps, though, I pondered almost wishfully, he lacks a little speed. I thought my reflexes were faster. This was important for in this department a tenth of a second means a point won or lost.

"Want to play a couple of practice sets?" Tony invited one afternoon.

I shook my head.

He seemed surprised at my refusal and countered with "Any particular reason?"

"None," I returned, "except that I prefer to save it for later. We'll be seeing a lot of each other."

"I'm sure of that," he concluded with a wide grin.

Readying myself for the "make or break" tour was my responsibility. Coordinating the tour was Kramer's job. Jack had plenty to do before getting the show on the road. Besides the various bookings, there was the advance publicity man, the special truck transporting our portable canvas court, equipment men, etc. The contestants were to travel in pairs;

Segura and I in one car, which I would drive, Trabert and Hartwig in another. Keep the competitors apart, was Kramer's credo.

A week before the starting date I cornered Segura for a talk. Little Pancho has a knack of getting out of answering direct questions by shoulder shrugs. He tried this with me, but I insisted he give it to me straight.

"What are they saying?" I kept repeating, meaning those close to the tennis picture.

"They're saying what you already know—that if you don't take this guy you're dead," he answered.

"What else?"

"You better stay in shape for this one."

"Anything more?"

He hesitated, finally speaking. "Many think you'll break fast on top, but once Tony learns the ropes he'll pass you."

I grinned. "Sounds like a horse race."

As the time narrowed before I was to fly to New York for the Madison Square Garden opening, I hardly had a minute to spare. Wolfgang Alexander Gerdes von Testa (for obvious reasons they call him Bud), my personal publicist, had lined up a series of press, radio, and TV interviews to be sandwiched between practices. After an appearance on the Groucho Marx Show a friend approached and commented, "You've changed, Pancho."

"For better or worse?" I asked.

"Better." He nodded emphatically. "Much better. You seem to like people now."

"I got to," I said. "I understand the world's full of 'em."

The day of departure for New York I took Henry into the bedroom, locking out the kids and the boxer pups.

"Something important to tell me?" she asked.

"An important goodbye."

"All goodbyes are that way, Richard."

My arms went around her. I have to be careful when I embrace her. Something hard can always crush something soft. She felt good and she smelled good. My heart rose like a fast elevator and seemed to finally stick in my throat.

I said, "I'll think of you."

She shook her dark head. "No. Think only one thing—to win."

"I'll win," I said.

"Stay cocky," she advised. "You can beat anyone in the world."

"Sure," I said, kissing her and then disentangling myself. "Keep hoping."

"I'll do better than that. I'll keep praying."

So it was off to New York.

I had no special strategy planned for Tony. I'd decided to make flash decisions influenced by whatever situations might arise, try to locate his armor chinks as the matches went from city to city. I thought: if I build up a lead, maybe this would intimidate him and give him an inferiority complex, making him happy to occasionally salvage a few sets.

In the New York debut, the shoe was nearly on the other foot. Tony, blistering the sidelines and passing me frequently at the net, grabbed the first two sets. Many people believe a tennis player has no time to think—that the next shot comes so quickly the mental strain is light. It isn't true. You simply think faster. My brain whirled like a roulette wheel when I was two sets down. Dreams were being shattered beyond repair; the future was there on the line. But when the wheel stopped and concentration began, the dream fragments were repaired and I ran out the final three sets. But it was a narrow squeak. I learned that to beat Tony I had to stay on top of him, forcing him into errors.

Every night I had to play it for keeps. Hell hath no fury like a tennis pro scorned financially, and I believe it was thoughts of the uneven gate division that spurred my game. It was give and take, and I gave and took the sweet rewards of knowing I could beat him just like I could anyone else in the world.

Segura was dealing out bad defeats to Rex Hartwig. They were playing under a point system, rather than by sets. The personable Australian would discuss his matches against little Pancho with rare displays of frankness, admitting the superiority of his opponent.

Asked once what he liked about the tour, he said, "Segura and the money."

I doubt if I could pay such a compliment to any man who was murdering me night after night.

Trabert, realizing that to lose on this major tour meant the end of big money offers, took his defeats hard. In one Eastern city, fed up with consecutive losses, he blurted to a newspaper scribe: "Gonzales tries every old pro trick in the game. He has no hesitation about trying to influence linesmen. He'll put his hands on his hips and turn around and look at them. He quick-serves me frequently. It's hard enough to return his serve when I'm ready, so when he tries this, I stop the ball. It may make me unpopular with the gallery, but I'm certainly not going to give him an additional advantage."

I am not going to elaborate on individual matches. But don't think I can't. I can separate each one in my mind and almost tell you the scores in any certain city. I can recall the highlights of each. The end of the American tour came at the La Jolla Beach and Tennis Club. Tony won the final match, 1-6, 6-2, 11-9.

I won the tour, 75 to 27.

Given a choice, I'd like to have shellacked him 102 to 0. Each one of the twenty-seven losses cut into me deeply. After suffering defeat, I'd either go to a bar and slowly sip a vodka

Future tennis champ at the age of five months.

One-year-old Pancho eyes camera sus-piciously.

Pancho's parents—Manuel and Carmen—on their tenth wedding anniversary.

Pancho Gonzales, age ten (top row, extreme left), receives first Communion at Holy Name Church, Los Angeles.

Pancho Gonzales and Johnny Shea (left) before the start of a boy's tournament.

Pancho relaxes with Arzy Kunz in Exposition Park Tennis Shop. Here is where Pancho kept one step ahead of the truant officers.

Chuck Pate, Pancho's closest friend, holds son who tries on one of Pancho's trophies for size. It was Pate who encouraged Pancho at the outset of his career.

Pancho fondles Blackie, the dog he was playing with the day he first met Henrietta. On the mantle are a few of his earlier trophies.

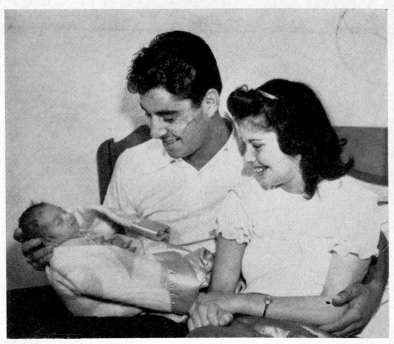

Pancho and Henrietta try to wake little Richard, their first child.

Japan gives Pancho the red-carpet treatment during a world pro tour.

Pancho collects tennis' most exclusive hardware—the National Cup. He defeated South Africa's Eric Sturgess (left) in finals.

Pancho and younger brother Ralph enjoy Pancho's victory over Frank Sedgman at the Youngsan, Korea, Tennis Courts.

Off the court Pancho keeps busy juicing up his hot rod.

Pancho catches up with a low volley.

The golden key to Juarez, Mexico, has just been presented to Pancho by Sr. Francisco Cuellar, executive secretary to Mayor Margarito Herrera of Juarez. Presentation was made during professional tennis matches played at El Paso (Tex.) Coliseum.

Humphrey Bogart and wife Lauren Bacall congratulate the two Panchos —Segura and Gonzales—at the Professional Tennis Tournament, Beverly Wilshire Hotel.

Ida Lupino presents trophies to winners of Pacific Coast Professional Doubles Championship at Beverly Wilshire Hotel.

Relaxing on plane between tours. Front (left to right): Pancho Gonzales, Jack Kramer, Pancho Segura. Rear (left to right): Jean Sedgman and Frank Sedgman.

The young Gonzaleses—Richard, Danny and Michael—have inherited many of their parents' features.

Gonzales family (left to right): Richard, Bertha, Joe Harless, brother-in-law, Margaret, Terry, Manuel. Front: Mr. and Mrs. Gonzales. (Ralph, another brother, not shown.)

The famed Gonzales serve, from start (top) to finish (bottom).

Pancho Gonzales about to take a backhand shot.

A backhand follow-through—Pancho-style.

Pancho readies himself to deliver world's fastest serve. Service has been clocked at 112 miles per hour.

or sit alone at a movie. I have a hell of a time taking defeat lightly. Some guys can brush it off like a fly. I can't.

Segura crushed Hartwig in the other singles attraction, and Trabert and Hartwig ruined Segura and me in the doubles. We played before more than 200,000 fans and traveled in 50,000 excess of 50,000 miles. The gross touched $175,000.

At the conclusion of the matches Tony revealed his fine sportsmanship by stating to Ned Cronin of the *Los Angeles Times:*

> "Gonzales is the greatest natural athlete tennis has ever known. The way he can move that 6-foot-3-inch frame of his around the court is almost unbelievable. He's just like a big cat. He instinctively does the right thing at the right time. Doesn't even have to stop to think.
>
> "Pancho's reflexes and reactions are God-given talents. He can be moving in one direction and in the split second it takes him to see that the ball is hit to his weak side, he's able to throw his physical mechanism in reverse and get to the ball in time to reach it with his racket.
>
> "The way he murders that tennis ball, I think his real name is Pancho Villa, not Gonzales."

Now that the feuding, fussing, and fighting is over and the tour a matter of record, I'd like to say this about Tony Trabert:

He's a born fighter who never gives up. You knock him down and he keeps getting to his feet. You may beat him, but you can't outgut him. I have nothing but the warmest regard for him.

When the tour ended, the letdown was terrific. Waking up in the same place every morning was a novelty. So was facing the day with no schedule. One thing that failed to add to my good humor was a short conversation I had with Ted Schroeder.

Ted had said, "How old are you now, Pancho?"

"I'm twenty-eight," I said.

"I'll give you one more year," Ted prophesied gloomily.

"One, hell!" I retorted. "I'm good for at least five."

Ted just puffed on his pipe and walked away.

I'll be good when I'm thirty-three. I'm going to make it. I simply won't accept the fact that my reflexes will slow, lead come into my legs, breathing be difficult before I reach that age. I keep thinking of Satchel Paige and how he pitches on and on, and of Jersey Joe Walcott who planned a ring comeback at fifty-one. I doubt if either of these venerables can hold physical fitness better than I.

Just when I was starting to relax by slow degrees, Jack Kramer came up with a brand-new idea—the Tournament of Champions. It was to be a round-robin affair held at the Los Angeles Tennis Club involving myself, Segura, Trabert, Sedgman, Hartwig and wonder of wonders, Jack Kramer, the old master himself. Doubles play was also scheduled. I was teamed with Kramer. Other duos entered were Sedgman-Segura and Trabert-Hartwig.

"If you win the singles, you'll get a cash prize of $1,750," Kramer informed. "The winning doubles team splits $1,000. The other competitors will be paid proportionally, depending, of course, on how they finish."

So there was to be no rest for the weary, but I wasn't complaining.

Once again I would be called upon to put forth every ounce of effort. Losing this one would be a loss of prestige not to mention the money. I couldn't afford either.

What especially pleased me was the chance to meet Jack Kramer in singles. By beating him here in his own back yard I could smother the voices of his loyal followers who still believed him the world's best. I wasn't worried. Jack was carrying too much weight and his arthritis prevented bending with his former grace and ease. Frank Sedgman was the real threat. He's always tough and unrelenting.

The tournament, played under the banner of a Catholic charity that shared in the proceeds, went according to form. When the final day of play arrived, both Sedgman and I had posted five wins. I experienced no end of trouble disposing of Segura and Trabert. Sedgman, to my surprise, swarmed all over Tony, dumping him 6-2, 6-1.

Both Segura and I really got in our licks on Kramer. Little Pancho handled him 6-3, 6-0, and I breezed past him 6-3, 6-3, never losing service. The first time I served he barely nicked the ball, and from that moment on I sensed he was but a shell of his once wonderful self. He still performed creditably in the doubles, making the most of his strong overhead, but singles is a vastly different game and Jack couldn't scamper around the court any more. The fighting heart was there on every point, but the legs failed to keep pace with his smouldering desire. The rewards of victory over Jack filled a long-time hungering, yet not with the satisfaction I had once supposed. Maybe I saw a crystal ball photo of myself in Jack, running to make retrieves that didn't quite come off.

Around the locker room where friendly bets are made, I found I was a 10-to-9 choice over Frank Sedgman. Many called him the "improved" Sedgman. Some smart bettors shied away from the action, calling it "a tossup."

Nearly three thousand fans were in the stands—paying top prices for seats—when we clashed. My serve was never sharper; I lost only three points on it the entire first set, which went to me, 9-7. Frank took the second set, 6-3. The final one was a 6-1 romp for me.

During the eight consecutive days of round-robin, sixteen thousand paid to see the pros play. The popularity of his attempt drew forth the statement from Jack: "This is going to be an annual affair. I'll be back with a bigger, and if possible, better Master's Classic next year."

Segura finished third, Trabert fourth, Hartwig fifth and Jack brought up the rear, not winning a match. Jack and I won the doubles with a three-win and one-lost record. Sedgman and Segura were next while Trabert-Hartwig occupied the cellar.

"Were you worried?" I asked Henry after the Sedgman match.

"Never," she said. "You're on top to stay."

I felt she was right.

Kramer talked considerably about his dismal showing. "I wasn't as bad as I looked," he claimed. "I was a year and a half out of tennis, and it's tough to come back. I'm still good for one more tour, although I would no longer consider casting myself in the top role. I intend to participate in the 1957 world tour against the thirty-six-year-old oldie, Pancho Segura."

Asked why he went into tennis promoting, Jack answered, "It wasn't a desire to make vast riches or be boss of pro tennis, but a deep-rooted wish to stay active in the sports picture. Right now the key to any tour is World Champ Gonzales, and I have him under a seven-year option. No tour can go without him."

He then added a sentence that started cash register bells clanging in my ears:

"Gonzales can't miss making one hundred thousand dollars next year."

I've never been to a concert. They tell me I'm missing the finest music in the world. I doubt it. I had heard it in the words of Jack Kramer.

10 I Begin to Think

Prejudice was a gigantic word for a youngster to grapple with. When I was about eleven years old I tried, and finally turned to Grandmother for help.

"What does it mean?" I asked her.

"People having unfair opinions against you."

Letting this sink in, I asked, "Against me? Why me?"

"Because you're a Mexican . . . a Mexican-American."

"Is that bad?"

"You are a good boy, Richard," she said, "and you have been spared certain unpleasantness. Someday, though, it might come."

Grandmother bade me sit down beside her. She was a small woman, and the chair in which she was sitting seemed to almost swallow her body. Her voice was soft, and her speech precise, and the words slowed along like a gentle river.

"You will know it, when it comes," she said. "Perhaps when you ask for a job . . . or the look in a policeman's eyes . . . the glances in the stores . . . the restaurants. It is worse in the heat of anger, when someone denounces you—calls you a Mexican and makes it sound ugly."

I frowned.

She reached out, putting her hand on top of mine. "Always control yourself inwardly," she advised. "Never lose your temper. Just gaze at your tormentor and conjure a picture."

"A picture?"

"Yes. Just imagine this man with his clothes off, standing in his long underwear."

I laughed.

"Laugh, that is good," she said. "That is what I want you to do. See the picture and laugh. He will look ridiculous, and if he appears ridiculous, his words will not hurt."

I never forgot this.

The favoring of one group of persons over another was something I wasn't conscious of for many years. Oh, I knew that the Mexicans' lot was a hard one, yet I never thought of them as children of a hybrid culture. I believed their troubles stemmed from being poor. I was wrong. We don't know what we haven't felt ourselves.

My youthful world was narrowly confined. Schools I attended had mixed enrollments. Invisible barriers were unknown because we didn't try to climb any racial fences, staying within our circle.

Not until a few years ago in Texas did I experience "the feeling." I went into a small restaurant with Pancho Segura while we were on tour. It was near the edge of town—a highway café. Although the place wasn't crowded, we sat for fifteen minutes, our hunger growing. Finally I called the proprietor. He slowly made his way to our table.

"Can we have some service?" I inquired politely.

He was a large, beet-complexioned man. All he said was "No. Not in my place."

"Isn't this a restaurant?" Segura asked.

"It sure is, Mister—and a good one," the owner declared.

"Well?" Segura said, waiting for further explanation.

"Can't you read?" he demanded.

"Read? Read what?" I asked, puzzled.

The proprietor jerked his thumb in the direction of the door. "Go outside and see what it says."

Segura volunteered. He returned a moment later, and although having the rather dark skin of a South American, the red showed through. "Let's go, Dick," he said, still standing.

"What does it say?"

"Nothing," he said hurriedly. "Let's go."

"Come on," I said. "Tell me."

He hesitated before answering, "No Mexicans served here."

"That's just what it means," chimed in the proprietor.

I indicated Segura. "This man is no Mexican."

"And this man," began Segura, pointing at me, "is the champion of the . . ."

"Never mind," I cut him off. "Let's go." I got up, tense, fingers balled tightly into fists. I peered for a full ten seconds into the proprietor's face and a picture, startlingly clear, formed in my mind. My tenseness vanished as I saw him in long underwear. He seemed ridiculous. We walked out. I heard him muttering to himself:

"Those Mexs' are all alike."

A month later in Los Angeles I mentioned the incident to my lawyer, Lou Warren.

"So it finally happened," he said slowly.

"What do you mean?"

"Look, Pancho," Lou paused to light a cigaret. "You've been lucky. You're a celebrity. You've escaped prejudice.

Any member of a minority group gets it in the neck at some
time or another. Now you know what it's like."

"It's not good," I said.

"It certainly isn't."

"How come I've escaped it, Lou?"

He blew a cloud of smoke into the air. "Happen to remember what Walter Winchell wrote about you?"

I couldn't.

"I'll tell you, then," Lou said. "Winchell wrote, 'Gonzales
is a man who prefers to have a hamburger and coke with his
old friends rather than a cocktail with a celebrity.' "

I smiled. "I can't say that isn't true."

Lou became serious. "That's one good reason you've escaped. You spend most of your time with friends. The rest of
the time where are you?" He answered his own question. "On
the courts swatting a tennis ball around." Lou ground out his
cigaret and glanced at me angrily.

"What are you mad about? What have I done?"

"Nothing," Lou said. "Absolute nothing. Maybe that's the
trouble."

"Lou . . . I don't follow you."

"Look, you're fast becoming an important man, an idol of
a lot of people, including thousands of kids. You endorse
things: what balls to use, what racket to play with, what shirt
to wear. But there's one thing you don't endorse, Pancho."

I remained silent.

"Your people."

"My people?"

"Yes. Your people—the Mexican-Americans. Their roots
grow in shallow soil here. They need help. Especially the
kids. They need understanding."

The trend of Lou's thinking started to jell. I remembered
the zoot-suiters, those gangs of Pachucos who gave the rest of

us a bad name. Why? I wondered. Driven by what motives?
They were always linked with frustration, conflict, violent
deeds, warped thinking. I glanced at Lou who was staring at
me, and I was sure he knew that the first buds of thinking
were beginning to sprout.

"What do you suggest I do?" I asked.

"Talk with some of the Mexican-American leaders in your
community. Men like Ignacio Lopez, publisher of the Spanish language newspaper, *El Espectador*, and Ed Roybal,
member of the Los Angeles City Council."

"And then?"

"Then it's up to you. You'll know your people better and
can help them get what they need most—sympathy and understanding. The younger generation will listen to you. You
can start them off on the right foot in life."

I thanked him for opening my eyes. "I'll try," I said, and
I meant it.

During the next week I called on a lot of people. Mostly,
I listened. I learned plenty. I began to understand the tough,
swaggering boy dressed in the long finger-tip coat with the
long hair swept back into a ducktail haircut, rocking impas-
sively on his triple-soled shoes, no expression on his brown
face. This was a uniform he was wearing, the sartorial and
physical mark of gangdom.

I wanted to know why he had to join a gang, why he had
to seek Panchuquitas—the female counterpart of his gang—
for companionship. Why all the cops were his enemies? What
he was trying to accomplish?

I found out.

When a German, Italian, Englishman, Swede, Frenchman,
or any other of the majority of foreigners come to this country, he becomes an American. It happens as fast as he learns
the customs and cultures of this nation. Not so with Mexi-

cans. They can be fourth generation, but if their skin is dark and if they bear a Spanish name, they are never accepted— they're always known as Mexicans.

They cry for recognition, a life without restrictions, equal rights, to find employment with chances for advancement. When they can't find a place in the American way of life, they are forced to resort to their own groups, their own behavior patterns which are neither American nor Mexican. And they become a clique widely separated from the majority of their countrymen.

This is a small but vicious group, numbering less than five per cent of the Mexican-American population. Yet, it is a group that attracts the attention of the press and the police and inadvertently smears the other ninety-five per cent until the blinded eyes of other Americans see all Mexicans in the light of trouble-makers.

They are created and weaned by unsympathetic teachers, suspicious police, wary merchants who think along lines of stolen goods. They are snubbed by superior-acting American kids. They are born in tenement sections—the sons and daughters of crop followers and track workers. Two strikes are against them the day they enter the world.

The Pachuco group hates the boys and girls of normal Mexican families who are bent on obtaining an education and the multi-benefits afforded by America. They call them "squares." Actually, the Pachucos aren't any worse than gangs of American juvenile delinquents who often spring from families that have given their children every advantage. But the Pachucos are the scapegoats, the cause of prejudice against hard-working Mexicans.

Yes, I learned plenty about my own people, and I resolved to do something to help, and I was thankful that Lou had opened my eyes.

Many of the Mexican-Americans are a bewildered, lost lot because they lack leadership. I wish my grandmother could address them. I can almost hear her say:

"Think of your tormentor standing in his long underwear . . ."

11 Life with a Wife

If you'd ask my wife the direct question: "What kind of a man is your husband?" she wouldn't smear my character. For two reasons: she's had only one husband, and she seldom uses profanity. Her answer, after a long moment of thought, might be, "Richard is kind, and he loves the children."

She's right on both counts. But there's more to the story. I'm stubborn, temperamental, and worst of all, a dictator. Most dictators meet a horrible fate. I'm the exception. I remain unscathed, head unbowed, issuing streams of dictums.

I get away with it. That's why I'm going to carefully spill black ink over this page of the book, making the excuse to Henry, "Very careless of me, wasn't it?"

Should she inquire what was on the marred page, I'd say, "My passionate declarations of love and fidelity toward you." She'd raise her eyes to me quizzically like a little chipmunk, not knowing whether or not to believe me. She's never sure because I'm a bedeviller. Next to tennis, I enjoy bedevilling her better than anything. Bedevilling is an art and a study, and I hold a master's degree.

I'll cite some examples.

Soon after Henry and I first started going together she invited me over to her house for dinner. "Mother's going out," she said, "and I'll whip something up in a hurry—nothing fancy, just pot luck."

Well, to make a long meal into a short story, I've never eaten such food (and probably never will again). I don't understand poetry, but if I did, I'd get poetic over that cooking. Each morsel of food was a delight. She must have spent hours in preparation, combed through cook book recipes, and enlisted the help of every woman in the neighborhood.

When the last bite went down and tried to find an unfilled place in my stomach, I pushed my chair back, clasped my hands gently over the bulge in my midsection and purred contentedly.

Henry's eyes sparkled delightedly. "Did you enjoy your dinner?" she casually inquired, waiting for the big compliment.

I said tonelessly, "It was a simple meal, but well-prepared."

See what I mean by bedevilling?

Sometimes Henry discloses, "We're invited to a party Saturday and I have nothing to wear."

"Good," I'll say. "You'll be sensational."

"May I buy a new dress?" she'll ask.

I'll shake my head sternly. "Of course not. We can't afford it right now."

A couple of hours before the stores close on Saturday, I'll say, "Show me the new dress you bought, Henry."

"New dress?" she'll sputter. "Why, you told me I couldn't have one. I distinctly heard you."

I'll act surprised. "Why, I don't remember saying anything like that," I'll claim, adding, "but of course you can buy one."

She'll rush to the store, just making it before they lock the doors, and invariably upon her return, say, "I'm so tired from last-minute shopping I won't enjoy the party."

But she does. Particularly if the new dress gets complimented.

Another incident, was the time a large mosquito buzzed through the bedroom. After arming myself with a wet towel, I said, "I'm an experienced mosquito-killer, a veteran of many Australian campaigns where they are more ferocious than anywhere else on earth, so listen to me. You stand in the middle of the room, acting as a decoy. You're sweet and taste good, you'll attract the mosquito. Then I'll get him."

She did as I bid, standing rigidly in the center of the room. I took careful aim and snapped her smartly on the rear with the wet towel.

"Ouch!" she screamed. "Are you sure the mosquito landed there?"

"Of course," I said. "Thanks for the cooperation. We make a good team. Like mixed doubles."

"I'm resigning from the team and you can get yourself a new partner," she announced, rubbing herself tenderly.

Being absolute monarch in my own home, I enforce a number of decrees. Chief among them is that Henry should never lounge around the dinner table after we've finished eating. Every dish must be washed first. I demand she be properly dressed for dinner at home—no robe, negligee, or sloppy attire. Another tyrannical edict is that no cheese in any shape or form shall be served in the house. I hate cheese. Maybe because I was once called a "cheese champion." Several times I've caught her sneaking it into cooked stuff—not because she loves it so—but it's merely a manifestation of her independent spirit. Also taboo in the food line is fresh bread.

All bread must be toasted. I'm not fussy about what kind is served, but it must be toasted.

We have no television squabbles. I like fights and Westerns; she watches movies and variety shows. Luckily, there are few schedule conflictions. If our set is off, Henry covers the screen with a special drapery. She says it looks like a great, dead face.

One of my bad habits is taking cigarets out of the mouths of athletic friends, even though I smoke when not training. I regularly sneak up behind Roxy Kunz, wife of my friend, Arzy Kunz, and remove her cigaret. Roxy hits a pretty hard forehand drive and it seems just a question of time before I get a closeup of the stroke.

Henry never smokes unless we have an argument. Then she'll light one after making sure I'm watching, while she struggles to keep from choking to death on smoke that goes down the wrong way. On the subject of arguments, we had a violent one several years ago. Henry very calmly told me that she read an article where a husband and wife each wrote down a list of each other's annoying habits, compared lists— and lived happily ever afterwards.

"Get me a pencil and paper," I said.

She did, found a pencil and paper for herself, and retreated to the dining room table to start writing. I was in the living room.

"Bring in your list when you finish," I said.

"See you in about two days," she called.

Ten minutes later she stood before me, paper in hand. "Your list ready?"

"Sure," I said. "Let's exchange."

She handed me hers. I handed her mine. Both were blank. We laughed for an hour. I never thought having a quarrel was very important. It's the ending that counts.

Another way I annoy Henry—not purposefully this time

—is to take Richey, my oldest son, over to Bob Duncan's garage and start tinkering on the hotrod. Richey helps. The boy is a natural mechanic. He even disassembles toy dime-store cars and, after sawing the bodies off, makes hotrods out of them. When we start working the time passes quickly and finally Henry locates us by telephone, often long after the dinner hour has passed. Incidentally, Richey's a good tennis prospect. Unlike most kids who just want to stand at the baseline and bang the ball, Richey prefers to serve. Somehow, he already senses that the serve is the important stroke to master.

Still a further reason why I'm a hard guy to live with is the humor gripping me when I wake up. You could shake me out of sleep, slip a million-dollar check into my hands, and I'd be mad. I want to wake up of my own accord, not by human voice, someone else's disturbing movement or an alarm clock.

I hate to poke around in stores. Everybody running helter skelter grabbing at things bothers me. I know next to nothing about shopping. The first time a salesman mentioned a layaway plan to me I thought he meant taking a trip with an unmarried woman. Henry buys all my clothes except my shoes. I figure that if a man walks on his own two feet he at least ought to pick out his own shoes to cover those same feet. Having your clothes bought for you has, I have learned, one distinct advantage. If anyone comments, "You look like a bum," all I have to do is jerk my thumb toward Henry. Sometimes her shoulders are broader than mine. They have to be.

Approximately once a year Henry and I hold a business conference; nothing of grave importance, mostly centering around what bills we've paid or have forgotten to pay. It's a good thing we're not joint proprietors of a store because we'd just ignore filing applications for various licenses. Henry loses and misplaces a lot of things such as car registration slips, and by the time she finds them we usually pay monetary penalties. I expect her to lose a lot of things and I write it off under the heading of WOMAN. A woman, I figure, loses about 5 per cent of everything, but as long as she doesn't lose respect for the man she married it's okay by me.

I'll always remember the day I came in the back door and heard the droning of women's voices in the sitting room. Henry was entertaining. Wondering what women talked about when they got together, I listened. Henry had the floor.

I heard her say, "Richard was never born. He was invented—by the man who gave us the wheel."

"Is he sweet?" someone asked her.

"He can be so aggravating at times," she said.

"You're lucky," said another voice. "Sam won't pay that much attention to me."

The chit chat continued unabated, and then someone addressed my Henry. "What's your formula for a successful wife, Henrietta?"

"Be independent," was her contribution. "Don't wait on them."

Now when I want to use it I've got a built-in moose call voice that can rattle the window panes. I amplified loudly, "Henry! I can't find the apple cider."

I peeked into the room and saw her jump like she'd been sitting in an electric chair when the switch was suddenly thrown.

"I'll find it for you, dear," she said, rushing into the kitchen.

I destroyed that theory in a hurry.

For me marital adjustment was hard, because, although I love life for two, I don't adjust easily. In fact, I just don't adjust. I'm like a stubborn rusted bolt on a weather-beaten hotrod that no wrench can turn. I won't even compromise. Poor

Henry's been forced to do all the adjusting. She's done a fine job. She's a gentle, understanding girl, made to order for my sudden whims and moods.

Few married men ever get spontaneous laughter like I receive from Henry while telling a joke. I have a guaranteed audience of one. I'm sure I fare better than the top comics in the nation. Their laughter rewards come after the punch line. Often it's a long wait during an involved story. I get mine during the telling of the joke, and when the punch line comes it doesn't matter for Henry's all laughed out by that time anyway. Henry says it's not the joke but the dramatics I go through telling it that panics her.

When chasing around the world on tennis tours, I seldom write a letter to Henry. Letters are tough for me. I perspire more composing a page than I do chasing a high lob on a real warm day. I prefer to use the telephone or the telegram.

My infrequent homecomings follow a pattern. They go this way:

"Why didn't you call or write you were coming?" Henry will say.

"Surprises like this keep you faithful," I'll joke.

"Hungry?" she'll ask.

"Always," I'll answer.

"For me?" she'll half-whisper and then in her loudest voice ask, "Or for a big, thick steak?"

"Mostly for you," I'll say, "but now that you mention a steak . . ."

She heads for the kitchen.

Every general runs the risk of an eventual Waterloo. My defeat was suffered in London at the capable hands of Charlotte Prenn, wife of Daniel Prenn, ex-German Davis-Cupper. At the insistence of our friends, the Prenns, Henry and I stayed with them during the playing of a professional tournament in London. This was the longest trip Henry had ever taken.

Charlotte Prenn is my self-appointed, in-absentia, mother and trainer. Living with her is like living in a training camp. She does everything but taste my food. She's a stickler for early retirement and a firm believer that husbands and wives should occupy separate bedrooms during training periods— and never the twain shall meet. It was an inflexible rule.

Henry and I were undergoing an enforced nightly separation. We were unable to muster any legitimate argument against these conditioning tactics because I kept advancing through tournament opposition. One night, Henry and I became conspirators.

"Bring some cards into my room and we'll play a little after the Prenns go to bed," I told her.

We bade our hosts goodnight. Henry went to her room. I went to mine. She allowed the Prenns a half hour to fall asleep before cautiously opening my door. We smiled. We felt good. We had pulled it off.

Suddenly the door swung open and there stood an infuriated Charlotte. Addressing Henrietta, she demanded, "What's the meaning of this?"

"Wh-why," Henry stammered, "I just dropped in for a game of cards."

"Cards, eh?" Charlotte said doubtingly. "Well, where are they?"

"Where is what?" Henry asked.

"The cards," Charlotte said impatiently. "Where are they?"

Henry looked at her empty hands. "Oh!" she exclaimed. "I guess I forgot them." She slunk to her room.

Charlotte's stringent training methods paid off when I won the tournament.

By all odds the worst habit my wife has and the one that can drive me raving mad is her littering the bed with a collection of stuffed animals. Imagine a man having to wade through an entire zoo every night before he can crawl between the sheets.

I repeat: this night-time menagerie of hers, headquartering on my bed, drives me crazy. Yet one thing puzzles me. Why do I keep buying them for her?

In March, 1952, a big, sticky, black blot was dropped on my private life. It stayed around until March, 1955, and I would enjoy eradicating it. It comes under the leading of "separation." Every day since that word was traded for a more compatible one called "reconciliation" I've been thankful and hope that I've now restored myself in Henry's eyes.

I could blame it on restless years when I was virtually exiled from chances at top tennis money; getting married too young; the curvaceous body and pretty face that trapped my thoughts; or a dozen other things. But what's the use of looking for or manufacturing excuses? Why did I have to prove to myself and everybody else that I was a man, when everybody, including me, knew it anyway? I don't really know the answer.

During those three unstable years I lived alone, going from apartment to apartment. Where I hung my tennis clothes and stored my rackets was home. I was drifting on a sea of impermanency, with no currents to carry me to the security of a port.

My attorney applied for a divorce. Henry refused. I didn't push it too hard. When I came to my senses the clouds of doubt vanished, scattered by rays of penetrating truth. I knew I loved Henry. Only Henry. I always would.

Her lawyer, Lew Warren, ended up as my lawyer, and I ended up with Henry. It was a very happy ending; far better than I deserved after three foolish years.

12 Pot Shots and Drop Shots

One standout advantage in being champion of the world in any sport is that people pay strict heed to whatever you may say. Attentive ears, hoping to pick up some fresh morsel direct from the playing fields, freeze in your direction like a pointer sighting quail. Reporters' pencils scribble into notebooks. Your utterances, profound or shallow, become grist for the newspaper presses.

Whether true or false, sports addicts believe that those who perform best know best. While the opinion of a champion may not be recorded for posterity, his views are at least stamped indelibly on the minds of the faithful. His name makes news. A gripe is a weak complaint if mouthed by a dub.

So in this chapter I'd like to touch on a variety of subjects, bearing down hard wth a spiked shoe, an iron fist, and leathery lungs.

Heading my Sound and Fury Department is temperament. Temperament is character; personality; mood changes. In tennis, temperament is like a girl's slip: it shows or doesn't show. Should it be visible, the player, according to audiences, is colorful. If it doesn't, he's drab, methodical. If it shows too much, the player is labeled unsportsmanlike.

King of the temperaments is Art Larsen, now sidelined from tournament play by a motor accident. Art does the unexpected, motivated by impulses. He's tense inside. His nervous system is a series of tautly drawn wires. Sometimes one snaps. Art has been known to hit a ball at a ball boy and climb into the stands bent on assault with a deadly weapon—a tennis racket.

Bob Falkenburg once sat down on Wimbledon's famed center court and before the astonished eyes of the fashionable crowd rocked back and forth in a fit of agony—actually a display of protest. The movement was called the "Wimbledon Roll."

Helen Wills walked off the court against Helen Jacobs during the finals of the Nationals, a mystery, never to this day satisfactorily solved.

Tom Falkenburg has thrown his racket against numerous backstops.

Earl Cochell's antics, touched off by temper explosions, got him suspended from U.S.L.T.A. competition.

Frankie Kovacs and Carl Earn, two gifted clowns, amuse the crowds with a steady stream of wisecracks—which relaxes them and often unnerves their professional foes.

But don't ever believe that the current crop of tennis players was the only group cornering the temperament market. Many years ago, Count Ludwig Salm of Austria, after being on the raw end of a number of bad calls, picked up the umpire's stand, carried it to a lake, and tossed the structure into the water. It just happened that the umpire who couldn't climb down in time got an unexpected bath.

Long before my time, Suzanne Lenglen, the fiery Frenchwoman, danced around the court in graceful gyrations, running the gamut of emotions. The late Bill Tilden related an amusing story about this talented lady stroker. French newspapers, nationalistic in spirit, began hinting that Lenglen might be able to beat any man in the world. Tilden happened to be in Paris, and he could read French. He invited her to play. Minus fanfare, they went to a court.

Bill waxed her, 6-0. Furious, Lenglen picked up her rackets, striding from the scene of the slaughter. Newsmen had gotten wind of the match, and rushing up to Lenglen inquired, "What happened?"

The French champion, her face flushed with humiliation, shrugged and said, "One of us won 6-0, but I can't remember who."

In 1956 staid Wimbledonians were shocked speechless when Vic Seixas made his final bid for the title. Seixas had broken Ken Rosewall's service twice in the fifth and final set to hold a 5-2 lead, having a semi-final victory within his grasp only to see the twenty-one-year-old Davis Cupper run the set out, 7-5.

Seixas, according to the British press, took his defeat badly and got the thirteen thousand center-court fans against him almost to a man. After the final point he hugged his head with his hands and arms, threw down his racket, refused to come up to the net, and it was Rosewall who crossed the net and patted the American sympathetically on the shoulder.

Seixas was charged with passing the umpire's chair without the customary "thank you" and other pleasantries. There were six line calls during the match disputed by Seixas.

Vic certainly wouldn't have won any popularity contest

during the long match interrupted during a two-hour rain-fall. The only contest Vic wanted to win involved tennis. His emotions simply broke the leashes of self-control. It was a heart-breaker. A man torn inside can't always smile through the tears and be the faultless little gentleman of British prep school traditions.

Temperament had cropped up where least expected—even off the court. Althea Gibson, one of the normally calmest women players, while on an around-the-world tour sponsored by the U. S. State Department, lost control of her emotional faculties on several occasions.

In England she snapped at a photographer, "Move back six feet! Don't make a close-up of me! I don't photograph well that way."

Another time she told a tennis writer, "Get one of the old stories out of the files on me and use it again."

In Paris a crew of Australian radiomen packed their wire recorder and departed after trying vainly to interview her.

I say this: A tennis player is entitled to temperament.

Nobody criticizes an actor or actress for temperamental outbursts. Is tennis so unrelated to the stage? On a court in an important match a player performs before thousands. He's crowd conscious; perhaps not of individual faces, but of the throng which includes the swelling tide of voices, the thunder of applause, the groans of sorrow. He becomes part athlete with a generous slice of ham thrown in.

He hasn't been trained before footlights. There's never been a Robert Montgomery coaching him. Emotions slipping out of him, even if in poor taste, are honest, unrehearsed.

Quite often a tennis player exhorts himself audibly to fight harder. Pancho Segura shakes a clenched fist, muttering the familiar war cry of "Come on, Pancho." I just scowl. They tell me it's a pretty black grimace. Other players get an emotional release by pounding their rackets into the net cords, banging them into the palms of hands, taking vicious swipes through the air at imaginary balls.

Turning back to the seemingly hostile and impatient re-actions of Althea Gibson, there are acceptable explanations. Her nine-month tour carried her from Mandalay to Trin-comales, the Middle East, Scandinavia and throughout Eu-rope. Such a tour can sorely test the stamina of a woman. Al-thea became road-weary. The strain rubbed her nerves raw. Is it any wonder then on a few occasions that she acted, let us say, as a human being?

Althea, spotlighted the moment she walks on a court, is constantly in the public eye. If she stubs her toe, it has news value. Due to racial barriers, she is a test case. She's the Jackie Robinson of tennis. Any person playing under similar con-ditions, unless he can completely mask every emotion, is apt to be caught with his humor down—and always at such times there is the ever-present sports scribe.

Some players, particularly the Australians, bottle their emotions, rarely letting them fizz over the surface. I don't know how they do it. Perhaps medical science should exam-ine their nerve structures. I do know this: They also win the Davis Cup.

Dick Savitt was none too popular in Australia for wran-gling with officials over whether to be allowed to wear spikes on slippery turf. Dick was fighting for his country, for the Davis Cup, for himself—and he wanted every advantage.

Questionable tennis tactics have been blasted by a num-ber of writers attempting to draw attention in their direc-tion. One of the most acid denunciations came from C. M. (Jimmy) Jones, former British Davis Cup player who now edits the influential *British Lawn Tennis Magazine*. His tar-get was the international tennis set.

Jones said points of tennis behavior which repelled him most were:

The practice of questioning umpire decisions "either verbally or with such anguished glances."

Bullying of ball boys and linesmen by international stars "until the unfortunate official is too scared to give a close decision against the star."

Delaying tactics when fatigued, which is "gamesmanship" carried to the point of almost cheating.

Slamming of balls into crowds, foul language, muttering, scowling.

I will try to answer Mr. Jones.

Of late years a popular pastime has been intimidation of officials who try to call 'em as they see 'em but too often miss 'em. I've done it myself. A scorching glare directed at a linesman, or to swing around and stare and shake the head incredulously, are all points, I think, which can aid the cause of victory. Speaking for the players, we figure that next time there may be slight intimidation on a close call—and the break may be ours.

Now I don't say this is highly proper; and maybe it isn't really too effective. But we're in there fighting for everything and it helps put on a show for the crowd. Years ago decisions were unquestioned. They were incontestable as if handed down by long-robed judges. Players took them with a smile. But I believe that audiences of today, if put to a vote, would prefer having us show our displeasure. At least it reveals we're not automatons.

Speaking of delaying tactics, no great wrongs are committed here when you consider that eleven men on a football team are stalling the closing minutes by running simple line plays and taking long counts in the huddle.

This brings to mind an interesting story. Constantin Tanasescu, who for nine years in his native Romania captured every tennis title in sight, turned professional and came to the United States in 1947. He now teaches in private schools and at the Rustic Canyon courts, Santa Monica. Tani said that in 1939 he reached the finals of the Italian International Championships in Rome. His opponent was Joseph Puncec of Yugoslavia. Puncec, large and powerful, was ranked No. 4 in the world.

Tani took the first two sets, 6-2, 6-3. The muscular Yugo-slavian, by hammering overheads and storming the net, chased Tani, whose height was a mere five feet six inches, all over the court to win the next two sets, 7-5 and 9-7. The tiny Romanian's legs were growing weaker and he was gasping for breath.

The crowd was wildly enthusiastic, all their sympathies centering on Tani. He was their darling, a midget contesting a giant—another David and Goliath story. Added to this, racial prejudice was in his favor, because Romanians speak a Latin tongue.

While sipping water and toweling himself, preparatory to starting the fifth and final set, Tani noticed half a dozen spectators who were sitting in the front row get up and leave. He thought that they, having sensed the handwriting on the wall, couldn't stand to see their favorite lose.

Tani walked wearily to the baseline to begin service when he heard an excited babble of voices and smelled smoke. A blaze broke out underneath the grandstand, clouds of smoke blowing over the court. The umpire motioned for him to hold up service. He quickly made for a chair. It felt wonderful to be sitting.

Puncec, observing him resting and getting his wind back, appealed to the umpire, contending that the smoke didn't matter—to resume the match. The umpire's decision was to wait. It took ten minutes to extinguish the flames whose origin was rubbish under the stands.

Turning to face the audience, Tani noticed that the front row of spectators who had walked out were now back in their

seats. Sly looks covered their faces and one of them winked
at him. Suddenly it became quite clear. They had started the
fire in order to provide him with a much-needed rest. He
smiled gratefully at them.

The respite helped. Playing like he had in the first set,
Tani took a 6-5 lead. Then he ran out of gas. One long rally
did it. His feet seemed glued to the court. He needed a rest.
He wanted to smell smoke again. He looked appealingly at
the stands, and the spectator who had winked shook his
head despairingly.

He learned later that guards had been posted beneath the
stadium.

Puncec won the set 8-6, and the match was his. Tani,
throughout the years, still thinks of the loyalty of that crowd.

American audiences are the fairest-minded. Pint-sized players—perennial underdogs against the giants—have long been
their favorites. They'll clap their hands until calloused for
Tiny Feliccimo Ampon of the Philippines. Bitsy Grant of
Atlanta was another darling of the gallery.

Some foreign audiences are replete with fierce nationalistic pride and take defeat of their countrymen the hard way.
Bill Tilden, up to the final stages of his life, ranted over crucial line calls against Wilmer Allison, U. S. Davis Cup team
member when he was playing against the French team in
Paris.

"The attitude of the French," Bill related, "at least in
those days, was to call them as they wanted to see them. Their
policy was to get away with anything they could and if they
couldn't, at least they tried."

Often I've sat in the stands listening to crowd reactions.
I've observed that when a player executes a spectacular shot,
his opponent who can't get near the ball comments in an au-
dible voice, "Pretty," or "Good shot," he is established in the
minds of the fans as a "good sport." Let me put you straight:

that guy is just voicing something stemming from sheer courtesy. Inside he's bleeding. Actually, he doesn't even think it was a good shot. He really blames himself for setting it up for his foe. Don't let those court commenters fool you. On the surface they may be gracious losers. In the locker room—if given the opportunity—they'd garrote their opponent with a long piece of racket gut.

The tableau that is enacted as players change courts is a grim one. They're like boxers going to neutral corners between rounds. Players go to opposite sides of the umpire's stand, wipe the handle of their racket, take a drink of water, towel, fidget, and rise to resume play. But never for a fleeting second do they look at their opponents sitting a few feet away. Above all, they never speak. No one breaks this unwritten law. Maybe some player should. It might jar your adversary out of the next game if you suddenly remarked, "Tony—how's your wife?"

Seldom does close friendship influence players. Most of them would crush their poor old mothers, 6-0, if she stood in the path of a championship. An exception was Ted Schroeder, when, as an amateur, the luck of the draw pitted him against his bosom pal, Jack Kramer. I never thought Ted went all-out to win. Ted was a fighter, a tiger when the chips were down, an inspirational player who never gave up. Against his close friend, Kramer, the spark was missing and Ted seemed to roll over and play dead.

Many persons ask "How come when a player turns professional he improves so rapidly?" and they point to Pancho Segura as an example. It's no secret that little Pancho during his amateur days was consistently beaten by players he could spot games to today. Why did he and others who have forsaken the amateur ranks skyrocket to sudden skill?

I'll tell you. The moment you turn professional you face only top-notch competition. There is no coasting through the opening rounds as in amateur tourneys. Each pro match is comparable to the finals of any amateur tournament. You can't afford to ease up. You must be sharp every day. You play more and in a more serious vein, with no time for clowning. Tennis to a pro becomes a business; your bread and butter and your future are wholly dependent upon it.

Another question constantly tossed at me is: "Could the old-time greats beat the modern players?"

The answer is a big and definite "NO."

Before the storm descends on my head, let me explain my reasoning. In the first place, I never saw any oldsters at their peak. Naturally names like Lacoste, Borotra, Brugnon, Cochet, Alonso, MacLaughlin, Billy and Wallace Johnson, Hunter, Bromwich, Crawford, Vines, and hundreds of others were headlines before my debut. From what I've been told and read of their terrific play I'm happy not to be a contemporary of most of them. I did tangle with Don Budge a number of times, but you can't in a strict sense of the word call him an old-timer. If you do, he'll take you to any court and make you eat the words. I've watched Bitsy Grant, Gilbert Hall, and Greg Mangin play when well over forty. I batted the ball around with Bill Tilden up to the time of his death.

The capabilities of these players were tremendous, their strokes almost lyrical. Then, you may pose the question, why couldn't they beat the players of today? And you may cite, "Didn't Bitsy Grant take a set from Art Larsen during an age vs. youth battle," and doesn't that prove something?

The answer is simple. The game has changed. The back court players have moved up to the firing line—the net— where points are won faster. The day of the long rally is doomed. The hard server and crisp volleyer wins today.

I maintain that had the tempo of tennis been speeded up in the early days nearly all those players who strung their rackets with the cobwebs of antiquity—particularly the ones with strong overheads—could have successfully made the adjustment. They were superb athletes, and men with such agility can always change their style. It was merely a different type of game then. A player stood in the back court and employed tactics. He was a field marshal plotting strategy on a small battle field. He searched for weaknesses, he analyzed, he mixed strokes. Only on a forcing shot would he go to the net. Even public court sages of that era would exhort, "Hit it to his backhand and go to the net." Now no excuse is needed for the forward surge.

Championship tennis today calls for the big serve, fast reflexes, some acrobatics. You smash the serve, rush the net. You keep your opponent off balance. It's a wide gulf of separation from the former game, but I say again that the stars of the past who had the physical equipment were perfectly capable of making the big change. I'm a guy who hates to take anything away from a memory, but I'm also a guy who dislikes building it into an incomparable legend.

Belittling newspapermen is the same as starting a shooting war with popguns against atomic weapons. The newspaper boys can give you the sharp end of the stick in print, even changing your character if they so choose. They can get very nasty if irked and take out on you grievances against management—chief of which is their being underpaid. They can make or break you, and it often depends on your personal press relations. I haven't been any champ at this but I'm improving. Regardless of what they think, this I've got to say that the majority of men assigned to tennis coverage in this nation don't know the basic difference between a racket and a shillelagh. There are, of course, exceptions.

Every tennis writer is a babe at a typewriter compared with Allison Danzig of the *New York Times,* that erudite, thorough and scrupulous coverer of tennis news. Mr. Danzig is a linguistic master of tennis verbiage. He puts the thrill of a football game into a tennis tournament writeup. His micro-scopic analysis of play includes a recapitulation where double faults, service aces, placements, etc., are accurately recorded. Reading him the day after a match is the same as going to a teacher and taking lessons on the revision of mistakes made.

The average tennis writer collects a batch of adjectives and tosses them carelessly into a couple of paragraphs. His clichés are so creaky it's a wonder the typewriter keys themselves don't revolt against the touch of his fingers.

I haven't the answer for tennis reporters' lack of understanding of the game. Newspapers do a fine job on football, baseball, basketball, and other sports of major public interest. Tennis, being on the minor side, isn't allowed the space of other sports, yet this isn't excusable for the poor writing job. Of late, tennis writers have discovered the word "clobbered," and few are the players suffering straight defeats who haven't been victimized by this over-used word.

The attitude of ranking players has changed during the last few decades. Not too many years ago when a ranking player led a mediocre player, 6-0, 5-0, needing only one game to end the uneven match, he generally made a couple of purposeful errors—trying not to be too obvious—in order to give his opponent the present of a game. Thus was a complete whitewash averted. This was known as a courtesy game.

None of this happens any more.

If a current player can crush another without giving up a single point, he'll do it gladly, swarming viciously to the attack, showing no mercy. It amounts to attitude, something vitally important to a person hoping to become a champion. Attitude must be implanted in the head and left to harden like cement. When it crystallizes all thoughts are molded with one objective in mind—to win and never let up. Giving a player a courtesy game might start a gradual disintegration of this hard structure and eventually prove symptomatic of a careless collapse of attitude. Trying for every point is the order of the day, at no time giving any quarter. Kill, kill, kill is the campaign cry among the top-raters.

Even when an outstanding player loses, he can't afford self-admission that he was beaten by a superior player. His offered excuses will be, "He was lucky," or "I was off my game," or "I didn't pace myself correctly," but never, never under any circumstances, "He's a better player."

You've got to beat it into your own head, washing contradictory thoughts out, except the solitary one, "I'll win." Otherwise, the proper attitude is lost. A man could repeatedly defeat you and give you an inferiority complex like Ted Schroeder nearly gave me. While you are congratulating the victor you must think, "Wait until next time . . . I'll get you." Maintaining this attitude is obligatory. All thought must be directed toward achieving victory with never a varying reflection that anybody in the whole wide world can beat you. If anybody should manage to beat you, why, all the breaks went to him—BUT WAIT UNTIL NEXT TIME . . .

While tennis courts in the United States aren't exactly vanishing like the buffalo did from the American scene, on the other hand they certainly aren't multiplying. Today, public park courts are the only citadels safe from the earth-gouging implements of tract-mad realtors. Everywhere, near or within the confines of cities, property values have soared. It stands to reason that small tennis clubs staggering along under heavy financial burdens can be tempted to throw in the sponge when approached by lucrative offers for their property. New clubs searching for sites would have to locate outside even the suburbian area.

Public parks are the last remaining fortresses whose bastions the armies of realtors will never scale. Yet in certain cities—Los Angeles for one—there is a dearth of these courts, with swarms of week-end players awaiting their turns. Here, new freeways snake through the city, and the builders' bulldozers have dug up some of the oldest courts.

What of the future of tennis and where will the courts of tomorrow be built? I predict rooftops. New York has already found this feasible. Any roof of adequate size with a flat surface can be remodeled into a hard-surface court. High backstops are a necessity, otherwise cascading tennis balls will add to the traffic confusion below. Courts nestled in the sky would be out of the realtor's reach and would keep pace with the increasing tennis population.

Tennis, although far from dying on the vine in the United States, isn't gaining proportionate to population increases. With large families the vogue, additional tennis players should be born. To inculcate more with the germ, I have a few suggestions. First, we need more group classes and organized tennis clinics. Then we haven't enough media of instruction. Some of this can arise from motion pictures and television programs, coaching by physical education instructors at all school levels. We also need provisions for free tennis equipment and free playing facilities for many who cannot afford such necessities.

Taking the boy off the pavement of city streets and transplanting him to the cement of the tennis courts goes a long way toward combating the seeds of juvenile delinquency. Good health, good sportsmanship, and good fun evolve from tennis. Buying a racket early for your child may spare yourself a lot of grief later.

A bad line call causes a player much mental suffering. Naturally, I mean when the call is against you. Defeat or victory can hinge on a line call. Out of all the bad calls I've ever received in my life, only one proved beneficial in the long run. This call came when I was playing Frank Sedgman, and a few seconds after the baseline man called "out," a woman's voice groaned, "No." Looking toward the direction of the voice I saw a pretty blonde head shaking negatively. The head, I recognized, belonged to Doris Day. Only a few nights before I had gone to a Western film and she was doing some singing on the other half of the double bill.

Several days later I received a letter which said:

Thanks for personally giving my husband and I a wonderful weekend.

Doris Day

Soon afterwards Henry and I met Doris and her husband, Marty Melcher, the film producer. We became firm friends.

Long before quiz shows were page one news in newspapers, I met a Hollywood actor's agent whose business was secondary to amassing tennis statistics. His name was Ben Pearson and he could qualify as a good Sunday player.

Over a glass of beer we talked the sport and he suddenly asked, "Do you think Beals C. Wright was ahead of his time?"

I didn't even know his time. In fact, I've never heard of Mr. Wright whom he explained was one of the early greats on the American tennis scene.

Commenting on the beer, Pearson said, "This is a very plebian drink compared with what Randolph Lycette drank while playing."

I learned that Randolph Lycette, a Britisher, downed champagne during his matches.

Then he said, "I wonder where Itchy is today?"

For my further edification I became acquainted with the fact that Ichiya Kumagae was an old-time Japanese Davis Cup member.

"Hell," I told him, "I'm lucky to go back to Don Budge."

As long as the name of Don Budge has come up, I might

as well speak of the night there was a leak in the dressing room of the Los Angeles Shrine Auditorium. It was the night that Don, described by sports reporters as "aging and faded," subdued me 6-2, 6-2, during a round robin affair. The leak was not in the ceiling or in a pipe. The leak was in the form of a report on my post-match conduct that escaped from the dressing room. Next day, much to my regret, a thousand people knew about it, including a segment of the movie colony, brought to the match by my friend Frank Feltrop, popular local pro.

When I went to shower I was in a miserable state of mind. Squarely in the middle of my black broodings lay my suitcase. Approaching the bag I drew back my foot kicking a hole right through the side of it. It helped. Then I saw a sign that said, NO VISITORS ALLOWED. I hauled off and punched it. This didn't help. The sign was made of steel.

Well do I remember the next day with my hand hurting and a friend calling up for a game. "Sorry," I told him, "I'm incapacitated."

"You're what?" he uttered, amazed because I've never been known to use many-syllabled words.

"Incapacitated," I repeated.

"What does that mean?" he asked.

"It's a common word," I stalled, trying to recall where I had picked it up and what was the definition.

My friend was insistent. "If it's so common," he said, "tell me the meaning."

"It means a sore hand," I said, punctuating the conversation by hanging up.

Cliff Sproul, one of the guiding hands of Australian Davis Cup players, opined that if the first twenty ranked U.S. tennis stars were pitted against a similar number of his countrymen, the Americans would come out ahead.

I agree with Cliff; and if matches were staged between the

first one hundred American players in the order of their rankings, against a similar number of any other nation in the world, we would beat them easily.

This hardly sparks the argument that as a tennis land we're fast becoming decadent.

American tennis is blessed with an equality of skills. Winning the Davis Cup requires two outstanding players. Two is all it takes. We don't have two. So Australia keeps the hunk of silver, but we're still the strongest tennis nation in the whole wide world.

Another fact I'd like to point up is that if the mantle of professionalism was removed from Jack Kramer, Tony Trabert and myself, wouldn't we, every year, be able to handle the dreaded boys from Down Under? I'd win both singles and doubles with Kramer. And there's the Cup. Substitute Tony for Jack and it would be the same. Use Tony for the two single matches and he might win one, or possibly both of them.

The obvious reason that Australia owns the Cup is because over here the outstanding players turn professional the moment a lucrative offer is dangled in front of them. You can't blame them. Money is a nice thing to have around.

It was while touring against Ken Rosewall that we played in Kansas City where I met a local obstetrician, Dr. Marcel Mooney. Dr. Mooney, who recalled "hitting a few balls" during his youthful days, remembered when a slice was known around the public courts as a cut shot.

I thought it was a good opportunity to discover what makes a man a tennis zealot, so I inquired: "Why did you come to the matches tonight?"

He explained:

"Watching tennis recaptures my youth . . . makes my pulses pound like an enthusiastic school boy again. When I watch you run and hit the ball, in spirit I am doing it with you. When you flub an easy shot I know your disappointment. When you scorch the sidelines I know your exultation. After a match I'm almost as tired as you from mentally playing every shot. Old tennis players never die. They just fade away into a grandstand seat. I think . . ."

The telephone rang. It was for Dr. Mooney. One of his patients was going to have a baby earlier than expected.

"I hope the new arrival has your forehand," said the doctor, slipping into his hat and coat.

13 The Lowdown on
Amateur Tennis

Let's journey down memory lane . . .

Remember the case of Wes Santee, former Kansas University track star and America's premier miler, who was banned for receiving overpayment of allowable expenses?

Remember the University of California at Los Angeles football recruiters accused of winking at various conference rules, resulting in a $93,000 fine and being placed on probation for three years?

Remember disciplinary measures taken against the University of Kentucky basketball team?

Remember relieving Jim Thorpe of his Olympic Games medals after discovery he had played some semi-professional baseball?

These alleged violations of the concepts of amateurism would pale into insignificance today if Dan Ferris, Avery

Brundage or Pincus Sober, the Kefauvers of the Amateur Athletic Union, investigated the amateur tennis situation.

They could obtain an injunction to prevent participation in all major tournaments by any of the first twenty ranking amateurs.

In tennis the difference between an amateur and a professional player is related to a phantom table. The amateur receives money under it, the professional over it. Today, a sought-after amateur can make from $8,000 to $10,000 yearly; yet in the eyes of the public he is pure as a virgin snow drift.

The United States Lawn Tennis Association, governing body of the sport, is blameless. The U.S.L.T.A. is composed of successful men of unassailable integrity. Rumors of the taints of amateurism have reached their ears. Some believe it. Others don't. Merely hearsay. Furthermore, it isn't their job to employ secret police or a spy system to track down such rumors. They merely impart the spirit and letter of the amateur code.

The code is antiquated. It provides ten dollars daily expense money.

Throw it out, I say; or make sweeping revisions.

Being that I'm in the playing end of the tennis business and not a member of its brain trust, I won't be presumptuous enough to name any cure-alls. However, unqualified as I may be, I'm bold enough to offer a few suggestions.

First, let me present, minus distortion, a clear-cut photo of amateur tennis today.

Put yourself in the role of the amateur. You're out of school and in the 20- to 30-year-old bracket. Perhaps you have a wife and a child or two. You may even have a grandmother who wants to take lessons from Mercer Beasley.

Maintaining a high ranking is synonymous with playing the Eastern tournament circuit. Europe too. Tennis becomes a grind.

Missing is the exuberance once derived from hitting a perfect crosscourt placement. The game becomes a chore. Believe me, a tennis player can suffer the same daily boredom as a CPA poring over columns of figures. Day after day he runs countless miles swinging at a wool-covered ball with strings made from a lamb's intestines. Physically, the game exacts its toll. He's dehydrated as a squeezed sponge. His feet take a terrific pounding on cement, clay, and the slightly kinder surface—grass. His sacroiliac is endangered. His disposition can sour after defeats. His heart and body are taxed to the limits of physical endurance.

While he may not realize it—he's in business. And he's putting as much into it as the business man carrying the brief case under his arm. Sometimes much more. Players are not the sons of the rich who burst upon a fashionable gathering wearing expensively tailored clothes and call: "Anyone for tennis?" More often, clad in a cheap T shirt and part woolen socks, they're the sons of the poor whose parents keep repeating: "What are you getting out of all this with your education when you could have been a banker?"

Undiluted amateurism implies that you cannot take one penny above the allotted expense money. On the ten-dollar-a-day allowance you're supposed to travel. Why, it almost means desertion and non-support to the wife left at home. So what recourse can you take? Tournament sponsors are bidding for your services. You become receptive to the highest bid offered.

You have ready excuses to make for yourself. Chiefly, you need the money. Sponsors can afford to pay; and after all, it's your name luring the customers.

The first time you take this money a few qualms of honesty prick you like dull needles. The second time you hurdle mental barriers much faster. It's becoming easier. The third time you merely extend your hand and wait for it to be filled.

The next step involves negotiations. You're getting real smart; and you finally realize that due to your high ranking you've got bargaining power. So you take the initiative. Instead of sticking a gun into some promoter's back and holding him up for more, you shove a tennis racket into his ribs and make your demands. Usually, the victim ups the ante.

True, that all this finagling might provide a modicum of business training, but think of the moral effect. You're not getting your money legally, coupled with the fact it's fraught with hypocrisy. A player seldom discusses his banditry with another player. One reason is a guilt complex. Don't bring it out into the open and it won't prick your conscience as strongly. Another is that some sponsors make you feel you got a better deal than the other players and it shouldn't be bandied about. This reminds me of a family hotel I knew about where each guest had a confidential rate which he or she thought particularly favored them. Had the matter been freely discussed, they would have unearthed the fact that everyone was being robbed.

Personally, I don't care to see an investigation of amateur tennis ending in a complete whitewashing of the sport. Unpleasant repercussions could kill off the game. From the amateur ranks spring the pros and, I hope, suitable opponents to challenge me. It's awful to run out of opponents. I know.

I don't believe an open tournament would solve anything either. Everybody who won prize money would end up a pro. The same pros would repeatedly take the cash prizes.

Amateur tennis can be a year-round activity if players want to follow the sun and are skilled enough to be in demand. You can chase the footsteps of Hugh Stewart or Tony Vincent and others—play America, Mexico, Europe, and even South America and Australia. But for the most part our amateurs compete only in the United States, with a stab at Wimbledon, the French Championships, and occasionally the Australian Championships.

It wouldn't be feasible to be in a business—even for themselves—and take that much time off. Frank Stranahan, as an amateur, could do it in golf, but no tennis player has the financial assets of this fine golfer. Dick Savitt and Ted Schroeder abandoned tennis careers for the world of business, and neither is employed by the type of organization where it's necessary to focus on their tennis reputations to boom sales.

Monetarily speaking, an athlete attending college is provided for through scholarships and jobs for just about his four school years. Couldn't the same be done for a tennis player? There must be some way he can receive monies while he isn't playing if he's expected to drop everything when the season opens.

In the last few decades the tennis scene has changed completely. Once the game belonged to the white flannel, polo-coated set. Not only did a player have to learn the book of social etiquette backwards, and grip a racket properly, he had to be able to lift a cup of tea without spilling a drop. Tennis and the Long Island horsey set were loving cousins. There was no so-called "wrong side of the tracks players." This group owned the tracks.

Came the evolution. Tennis became the people's game. Public park courts mushroomed. Expensive clothes for players were unnecessary. All a man needed was a drugstore T shirt, a pair of cheap shorts, dime-store socks and shoes that could be adhesive-patched if your toes broke through, or vulcanized on the soles when your feet showed.

Audiences became plebeian, more demonstrative. Where formerly ripples of applause rewarded shotmakers, there were now roars of appreciation from shirtsleeved masses, and even choruses of boos directed at bad calls.

Tennis became of age and widespread in popularity. Then the attendant evil followed—bidding for the services of the players. I don't know who was first guilty. That is of small concern. Once the cash payments gained momentum, they fanned out in all directions.

True enough, tennis players get a lot of free things in life —food, rackets, balls, strings, shirts, shoes, sweaters, lodging, and lots of advice, none of which helps them later in life. In the life of each tennis player there's the point of no return. Here, you either drop the sport and concentrate on making a livelihood or stick with it, trying to live off its sometimes frugal returns.

At the frayed edge of an amateur career, when a player touches the age of thirty, it's later than he thinks. To regress to the business world and try to carve a niche for himself is a mammoth undertaking. He's already lost ten productive years. He's too old to start at the bottom, too inexperienced to hold down a top position. All he's got to show for his efforts is a scrapbook, blistered feet, and tarnished trophies.

Please bear in mind I'm not turning copper and blowing the whistle on amateur tennis. It's still the purist of the popular spectator sports. Only a handful of amateurs in tennis really make any money. Total these against the earnings of football, basketball, and track athletes. The difference is monumental.

What's to be done about it?

Let's face up to the situation. No circumvention. Shouldn't we make a choice between honesty and hypocrisy? But not a compromise. Otherwise, the evil side can undermine the strong side until the roots decay and collapse the entire structure.

The line of demarcation between pros and amateurs is wavy and vacillating. A rigid line with no overstepping is necessary.

To make a sincere start, let's compile an amateur tennis code that makes sense.

14 The Day I Exploded

Much credit must be given to Jack Kramer, who, operating without a medical license, and using a checkbook instead of a scalpel, disjoined the Australian "tennis twins"—Ken Rosewall and Lew Hoad.

For two frustrating years, Kramer had been trying to snare Rosewall and his Australian partner, Hoad, but the youngsters preferred to help keep the Davis Cup in Australia rather than cash big pro paychecks. But now he had Rosewall, half of the famed combination, and a worthy headliner for his new pro tour.

Hoad turned down cold Jack's fat offer which would have netted him $67,500, tax-free, at the end of two years. His reasons appeared to be nationalism and the desire to score the grand slam of tennis—winning all four major tournaments.

To me, the refusal was fantastic. Maybe it's the hard core

of the old pro inside of me that cannot yield to such thinking. Since Lawyer Lou Warren is shaping my mind toward an investment consciousness, I immediately whipped out a pencil and started figuring 5 per cent of $67,500. Three sheets of paper and plenty of erasures later, I found it amounted to $3,375 per year interest on the earnings that might have been. That would buy Lew's wife, Jennifer, a barrel of nylons.

But Kramer *did* bag Rosewall, who had beaten Hoad in their last three encounters, including the U. S. National Singles. Tennis forecasters felt that at long last he had come of age in assuming superiority over his blond teammate. When the dark-haired, slightly built youth affixed his signature to Kramer's contract, he assured himself of a nice income. In addition to the $65,000 guarantee for a period covering thirteen months, he was promised 25 per cent of all receipts over the $300,000 mark, plus a 5 per cent bonus and an option on a new $25,000 contract if he beat me. If he beat me he would be crowned king of the pros. If . . .

Here for the first time in my professional life I was about to face an opponent minus my usual "I-can-beat-anyone-in-the-world" attitude. Two contributing factors influenced my thinking. Factor One—I was dead tired. Since the beginning of the tour against Trabert in 1956, I had been on a tennis treadmill that took me to South America, Europe, South Africa, New Zealand, Australia, and finally home to Los Angeles, then after barely three weeks' rest I was to wing back to Australia again to play eleven matches against Rosewall, compete in a professional round-robin championship, and then return to the United States to wind up a 100-match 1957 tour against Ken.

Factor Two—my hand. A cyst the size of a half-dollar had formed beneath the surface of the palm of my racket hand.

Believe me, it was painful. Several newspapers hinted my career might end.

The moment I reached Los Angeles, I made an appointment with Dr. Omar Fareed, whom Jack Kramer had recommended. His diagnosis indicated the cyst was attached to important tendons and removal might mean loss of power in my grip. He started a series of injections to dissolve the lumpy mass. I began worrying, which was something new for me. Rest was out of the question. Tour dates were being booked. The show must go on, even though I might end up playing the role of chief tragedian.

Over one hundred people telephoned, keeping Henry busy as a switchboard operator. Sister Margaret Evelyn of the Saint Bridget's School, where our children attend, told us she was having a Mass said and novenas made for my recovery. Gradually the cyst decreased to the size of a nickel which prompted some wag to remark, "It's shrinking in value like the American dollar."

I left for Australia, realizing that my hand was still sore and I'd have to play with a pad on it for protection. First stop was Honolulu, and flying over the Pacific allowed me much time to think of Ken Rosewall. He certainly didn't pack the power game of any of the big names in tennis. Ken weighed 142 pounds, and was barely five feet seven inches tall. His tennis reminded me of a fencer, thrusting, parrying, nimbly dancing. Strategy was his forte. Strategy, I thought, can be overcome by sheer power.

His stroking was flawless. He was exactly what the instructor ordered. He played the game literally the way it was taught. His backhand, slightly undercut, looked stronger than his forehand. But that was deceptive. He took his forehand shots nicely on the rise with pace. His serve held no terrors. Yet it was effortless and well placed.

Reporters rushed to interview me in Australia. "Rosewall is in better condition than I am," I told them, "but I will guarantee he won't be for long." Queried as to whether I thought I'd beat him, my answer was, "Everything being equal, a good big man can beat a good little man."

Kramer, writing in the *Melbourne Argus,* said, "Off the record, Gonzales appears a likely winner, but stand by for an upset."

The Australian Nationals were ending and Lew Hoad was a surprise loser to Neale Fraser in the semi-finals. Hoad was in great pain during the match, but he offered no excuses. Lew's trouble was thought to be a slipped disc, but a specialist later identified it as a strained ligament in the lower part of his back. It was necessary to encase his aching back in a sixteen-pound cast, and this raised a big question mark about the blond bomber's future on the courts. A recurrence of the trouble might jeopardize Hoad's chances of cashing in with the pros. So painful was the injury that his wife, Jennifer, had to put on his socks and shoes for him before the contest against Fraser.

In the opening match against Rosewall at Kooyong Stadium, Melbourne, I won 6-3, 3-6, 6-3, 1-6, 9-7, during 125 minutes of torrid play. Ken came right back the next night and dumped me 7-5, 6-4, 14-12. He seemed more assured and dictated matters right from the start. His reflexes were razor-sharp. It became touch and go. We had another marathon match lasting three and one-half hours. I took it 3-6, 6-3, 11-9, 1-6, 15-13.

What surprised me was the ease with which he was returning my service. Waiting for it, he reminded me of a coiled spring. Then suddenly he would whirl in the direction of the ball. Aces against Trabert were fairly common. Not so now.

Crowds were beating all expectations. Kramer wore an

almost continuous smile. For the first six matches gross receipts totaled $113,000. Five of the outdoor matches were sellouts. Rain dampened the sixth. For the Kooyong appearances the gate touched $42,000. It looked to me like Ken would realize $100,000 for the tour. Quoting from a letter Kramer's wife, Gloria, wrote to Jeane Hoffman, the *Los Angeles Times* sports scribe:

> "It's a smash success. There is a bigger demand for seats than there are seats available, so they sell standing room only— except that it's really sitting room—and fans sit on the grass in front of the regular seats. Everything the boys do down here is front page news. In fact, even Frank Sinatra's arrival took a secondary spot!"

The drawing power of professional tennis moved Donald F. Ferguson, ruling voice of the Australian Amateur Tennis Association, to complain that Kramer was dipping into the ranks of amateurs for his players, that he was robbing the country of tennis power. He also rebuked the owners of Kooyong Stadium for renting the facilities to our troupe. It was apparent that his attitude was crystallized by falling gate receipts at the Australian Nationals with no Rosewall entry and Hoad failing to reach the finals. Seven thousand was the top crowd.

The attack on professional tennis was launched at the annual interstate tennis conference held in Melbourne. Several delegates urged that amateur associations should stop cooperating with touring professionals. G. A. Bitcon proposed that no professional matches should be allowed on any State Association courts within a month before, or until fourteen days after, a national championship, Davis Cup, or international matches.

Another delegate, D. M. Frankenburg, said: "We should not allow the immediate dazzle of gold from the professionals to blind us in our long-range vision. We should ask ourselves: 'Are we helping to develop professional tennis to the detriment of the amateur game?' They make large amounts of money from our courts, whereas if they were pushed into other stadia they would make only half the money and be able to offer only half the inducements to our young players to turn professional. It hurts me to see them get rich by exploiting the amenities that amateur officials have worked to build up."

Delegate A. R. Colvin, a man not given to verbosity, summed up the success of the pros by stating: "A polished acting society will always make more money than a repertory company."

All this talk sounds too much like our troupe is composed of plunderers and cradle-snatchers. In defense of our actions, let me say that Jack Kramer presented the Victorian Tennis Association with $3,200 from the matches in Melbourne and the N. S. W. body received $6,000. Also, Jack made sizeable donations to the Lawn Tennis Association junior development plan and a project which operates in the Hardcourt Associations.

No fanatical tennis partisans exist anywhere in the world like the Australians. They have rabid, shirtsleeved, cheering crowds comparable to Milwaukee's amazing baseball fans. It was to be assumed that I'd be on the short end of the applause. Ken was one of the real sports heroes of the country, and my height stacked up against his turned it into a midget-giant struggle.

Most of the Australian sporting public are fair-minded. A small percentage are wildly boisterous, completely lacking control—the real noise-making, razzing kind. These antics are embarrassing to the majority who try hushing them up and later apologize to the competitors.

While competing in the AMPOL Tournament of Champions in Adelaide, South Australia, a spectator got my goat.

Fifteen thousand people were watching the pros in a round-robin style of play. Though it was night, the temperature hovered around 105 degrees. Humidity was high. Some of the fans were sopping up beer, and beer and humidity and tennis just don't seem to mix.

From the outset of the tour several newspapers had become habitual misquoters. Every statement I made was twisted until they had the overtones of braggadocio. One of the spectators with a retentive memory was catcalling some of the quotes. His voice echoed around the court. The constant heckling was bearing down heavily on my frayed nerves and over-tennised condition.

I walked in front of a section holding about five thousand people, where somewhere the heckler was concealed, and called: "Listen, Horsehead, you're very brave hiding among all those people. Why don't you come down here where I can see you?"

Of course he didn't move.

Later, Jack Kramer said he would probably fine me and demand an apology. He did neither. We both let the incident slide.

As the match progressed, I won the first two sets and it was 4-all in the fourth with game-point on my service. I faulted and threw the ball into the air for the second serve. Just before it fell a voice boomed, "Go!" I let the ball drop, stood and waited. General bedlam broke out in the stands while hundreds tried to quiet the shouter. Finally I served again and double-faulted. I lost the game.

I was thoroughly disgusted with myself as I walked toward the umpire's stand to change courts. My head was down and I was tense and brooding, seething with suppressed wrath. I looked up. Directly in front of me was a dead microphone, the only thing around that couldn't sue me if I hit it.

I slugged it with my racket—hard. I had to take out my

feelings and release my emotions on something. I like to think I'm human.

I lost the set, and in the final set Ken played magnificently to take the match.

Then the press really loused things up, claiming: "Gonzales turned and hurled his racket at the umpire box. It struck with such force it hit a microphone and bounced into the stands."

This was unkind and untrue. It happened as I described it. While I admit my outburst was wrong, I don't think I shattered tennis etiquette too severely. Once in a while an emotion has to slip out. At least I didn't spit at the crowd like Ted Williams did in baseball.

Back in Los Angeles, Henry commented, "If I know my husband, he called the heckler a much worse name than 'Horsehead'." Well, I admit I thought of a worse name but I didn't use it.

Pancho Segura won the tournament. I'm glad he did. He won $4,500 in cash and an immeasurable amount of confidence. I played Rosewall once more before returning to the United States. He smothered me, 6-1, 6-4, 6-2. I was tired and weary, and my hand was hurting, but I got out of Australia with a 7 to 4 lead. I felt fortunate.

And, oh, yes—Jack Kramer paid for the busted mike.

A few days before I left Australia a newspaper approached me and offered to pay for several byline articles. Believing it a good chance for a final, accurate interview, I accepted. Here are a few excerpts:

"Now that I am calmed down over the Adelaide incident, I don't want Australians to think I am a knocker of the greatest sports nation in the world. Please don't put me in the same class as Art Larsen and Dick Savitt who squealed when they went back to the States that they would never return to

Australia. Apart from the lame brains in Adelaide, the Australian public has been wonderful to me.

"I've tried to repay them by playing the best tennis I can. The truth is I've never had it better than in Australia. In one month here I've put away more money than I extracted from Jack Kramer in five whole months last year for blasting Tony Trabert in North America.

"I made one hundred thousand dollars in my first pro year in 1950, but I played fast and wild with it. Then came lean years. Now I aim to get out of pro tennis with around two hundred thousand dollars which should give me a good income for life.

"Only Ken Rosewall stands in my way this year, and after that looms Lew Hoad. If you want to know something, I think I am lucky Rosewall is only half my size. Every time he returns a well-placed first service it amazes me. He ought to be an inspiration to all the small players in the world."

For the first time in my life, while riding on a plane from Honolulu to Los Angeles, I took sleeping pills. I felt no effects. Upon arrival in Los Angeles I made several important appointments, including one with my income tax man and another with Lou Warren. I kept neither. The sleeping pills struck with delayed action, delivering a punch that knocked me out for eighteen hours. At a press luncheon the following day everyone said, "You look great. Refreshed and rested." I should. Eighteen solid hours of sleep is a precious thing. Yet I was worried about my hand. I told everyone: "It feels fine." It didn't. But, again, there was no time for rest. The test was coming February 18 in Madison Square Garden.

The Garden held 11,416 spectators on the night our tour made its American debut. They paid from three to six dollars a seat. I wanted to give them more than a faulty, sore-handed exhibition. I believe I did. I put a pad over my cyst, put desire in my heart, and played with a minimum of errors, trouncing Ken, 6-2, 6-4, 6-2.

My hand felt pretty fair. Confidence, big, wonderful gobs of it—if such a delightful thing can come in gobs—returned. I strongly felt I'd win the tour. The canvas-covered court was lightning fast and made to order for my serve and volley. If the serve and volley worked well, I figured I wouldn't have to fear my opponents' ground strokes. Still, I didn't think I'd beat Ken as easily as I handled Tony Trabert. Tony and Ken clashed in Australia and Ken won the decision in straight sets, taking up where he left off in Davis Cup play and the U. S. Singles. Ken moves better than Tony.

An amateur switching to the pro game indoors always is at a disadvantage. The artificial lighting, the strange footing on the canvas court, and so many other first-time experiences stack up against him. But then there was my damaged hand. I wondered if it could balance the scale.

15 And Now, Lew Hoad

As my tour with Ken Rosewall progressed over wearying miles of travel, from city to city, from arena to arena, I gradually assumed complete mastery over my Australian foe; and by the time our troupe reached Bakersfield, California, to close out the long journey, the score stood 51-26 in my favor. I was very tired, very happy, very gratified.

Plans had been made for scheduling the tour in South and Central America, but I begged off. I wanted to stay at home, rest, and begin knowing my family again. Ken, though, was committed to finish the grind. I felt sure that he was going to be relieved at my absence on the opposite side of the net.

He may have been somewhat discouraged, yet he never showed it. In Princeton, New Jersey, he told a newspaper scribe, "Pancho just doesn't seem to have any bad nights. It's not human. He's not human. He's always tough. I have to work like crazy in every match, and it's only when I'm playing extremely well that I'm able to pull off a win. Somebody ought to define and spell the word 'slump' for Pancho. I don't think he understands it."

Jokingly, Ken told reporters that he grows fearful when someone in the stands provokes me. "It is then," he commented, "that Gonzales takes it out on me, the innocent bystander, and practically blows me off the court."

He was referring to one night in Boston, a night when I thought the old saying about "banned in Boston" might be applied to me as well as book censorship. I made for a heckler in the grandstand, but I'm happy to say I was restrained. Too many people enjoy suing these days.

We interrupted our tour to compete in the National Professional Championships, in Cleveland. I got a respite from Ken. Segura neatly arranged this by eliminating him. After a first round bye, I handled Frank Parker, 6-2, 6-3; Tony Trabert, in a battle down to the wire, 3-6, 8-6, 11-9, and went on to defeat Segura in the finals, 7-5, 4-6, 6-3, 6-1.

At this point I want to contradict a rumor that reached my ears at least a dozen times. It's been said that after losing a particular hectic match to Ken I jumped into one of our tour cars without waiting for the customary passengers, driving alone and in anger to the next city—thus fouling up our transportation and creating an over-crowded situation. Added to this were whispers that I was trying to leave town as fast as possible after losing.

This rumor is untrue. I believe I know its origin. One afternoon after Ken beat me, I was anxious to get started for the next town and I hurried everybody up, nearly pulling Segura out of the shower before he was finished. I had a reason, childish as it might be. In my mind the sooner I got to the next city, the sooner I could avenge my defeat. Crazy thinking? Sure it was, but it was the motivation for my hurry and too-fast driving.

While we were winding up the tour I was taking a long-range look across the Atlantic at the forthcoming Wimbledon tournament, sharing Jack Kramer's worries about the dwindling class of first-rate amateur competitors. Jack expressed sorrow that America's first ten players were the weakest he had seen in fifteen years. For once I was forced to agree with him. Vic Seixas, an accomplished Internationalist, was too old; Ham Richardson was wrapped up in his studies; crafty Budge Patty was over the hill; and Herb Flam was unable to climb the same hill.

Both of us agreed that the only hopeful prospect in our country was Alex Olmeda, a student at the University of Southern California. Alex is a good future bet. He even scowls like an old pro. However, Alex is from Peru. America has no fine prospect unless there's one hiding out in the woods.

On the other hand, Australia, as usual, boasted of an abundance of fine players, like Ashley Cooper, Mal Anderson, Neal Fraser, Rod Laver, Bob Mark, Mervyn Rose, Bob Emerson. Any one of these could rise to greatness. The Aussies seem to turn them out like a factory and must surely have a network of conveyor belts leading from the crib to the court. Still there was one player head and shoulders above the pack, and that was Lew Hoad, the powerful, chief guardian of the Davis Cup. Hoad was the star, if not sometimes recalcitrant, pupil of Harry Hopman.

As previously stated, Lew had been stricken with the miseries and during 1957 his tennis was only spotty. I had an idea he was saving himself for an all-out effort at Wimbledon. I sincerely hoped so. The gap was wide between Lew and his countrymen. If Lew lost at Wimbledon, or for that matter even if he won and refused to turn professional, 1958 promised to be a dull year for World Tennis, Inc., and Pancho Gonzales.

Interviewed by Jeane Hoffman, of the *Los Angeles Times,* Jack aired his views:

"Overall," he said, "there's nothing wrong with the tennis picture today. Tennis, on a sporting goods basis, is doing greater than ever. More people are playing it. But either the kids of top ability are going into other sports, or they aren't getting the right foundation. A degree of it is my fault; I helped popularize the boom serve and net game, and too many kids start out that way now. You've got to master the fundamental strokes and baseline play first."

Kramer lamented that "Even Don Budge, who's forty-two, can take the measure of some of the kids coming up today. It's a rough situation. I've been accused of whipping the cream off America's amateur tennis, but at the moment there's no cream to skim."

So it was squarely up to Lew Hoad. Only Lew could add more sugar to the already rich, creamy confection that was professional tennis. Without Lew the confection might go stale. Of course it was also up to Jack Kramer; up to him to come through with an offer that could not be refused. I had every confidence in Jack. Combine a bankroll with personal magnetism, add a dash of superlative salesmanship, and the merger is nearly unbeatable. It was Hoad winning Wimbledon, or bust, as far as my 1958 plans were concerned.

First round play of the 1957 Wimbledon tourney provided no test for the stocky Aussie. He took Pierre Darmon of France in straight sets, 6-2, 6-4, 6-3. The second round saw Lew score another easy victory as he raced through Roger Fancutt of South Africa, 6-4, 6-2, 6-1. He was still untested. The third round found Lew stroking sharply and crushing Johnny Lesch, a UCLA student, 6-3, 9-7, 6-4.

Fellow-traveling Australians were now crowding the brackets, and all of them loomed as severe roadblocks along Hoad's pathway. Several of them had beaten him in major tournaments. Yet, when he swept aside the challenge of one of them —Roy Emerson—6-4, 6-4, 6-2 to gain the quarter-finals, I breathed easier.

Mervyn Rose, another of the Aussie contingent, was next on the docket. Mervyn, who had been playing in U. S. winter tournaments, was always tough. Lew mangled him, 6-4, 4-6, 10-8, 6-3, and was scheduled to square off in the semis against Sweden's Sven Davidson, conqueror of Vic Scixas. Lew took the sometimes brilliant Swede, 6-4, 6-4, 7-5. He was ready for the finals against still another Aussie, Ashley Cooper, who had polished off the retrieving Herbie Flam in straight sets, and countryman Neal Fraser, three sets to one.

Cooper was a good-looking, power-type player. Bobby-soxers sigh at the sight of him. Hoad did anything but sigh. At his tremendous best, his attacking game completely demoralized Cooper. Twice Lew's stinging shots sent the racket flying from the hand of his rival. Gardnar Mulloy, dean of American players and 1957 Wimbledon doubles winner with Budge Patty, characterized him in *World Tennis* as "a reminder of one of Disney's animated rabbits whose feet spin when running at top speed."

It required only fifty-five minutes for Hoad to do the job. Cooper was beaten, 6-2, 6-1, 6-2. I believe Lew, in winning his second consecutive Wimbledon, maintained a calmer attitude on that memorable day than I did. I paced. I fretted. I kept bothering newspaper sports desks by constantly calling in for results. Although Davis Cup play and the U. S. Nationals were still on Lew's tennis agenda, he was now fair game for Jack Kramer's offers.

Lured to New York, Hoad signed with Jack, much to the consternation of the Australian Lawn Tennis Association. That august body had been counting heavily on Lew defending the Cup. Lew received a guarantee of $125,000 against a 20 per cent gross for a two-year contract.

Australian sports columnist Harry Green, long a protagonist of pure amateurism in tennis, exploded in the *Melbourne Sun* that Lew's action had toppled the Davis Cup from the very insecure perch of the world's top tennis fixture.

"From here—at least for several years—the Davis Cup is strictly for second-raters," he declared.

Bitterly he wrote: "How can the challenge round be the test of the world's tennis supremacy when hardly any of its contestants are among the world's top ten?"

"Surely, the only real battle could be between Hoad, Ken Rosewall, and Frank Sedgman, representing Australia, and Richard Gonzales, Tony Trabert, and Jack Kramer for the United States. If any of these six players are at the challenge round, it will be as newspaper or radio commentators. Out on the court will be players either too young or not just good enough for the professional game."

Meanwhile, Mrs. Bonnie Hoad, mother of the twice-crowned Wimbledon champion, admitted that it seemed a miracle that her twenty-two-year-old son was even playing. She revealed that Melbourne doctors who examined him six months earlier placed him under a sentence of tennis death. Medicos believed that Lew, close to the peak of his career, was slated never to hold a racket again.

Mrs. Hoad further disclosed that after the national titles in Melbourne in January, 1957, doctors told her that her son's injured back would forever stop him playing. "Instead of taking this advice," Mrs. Hoad said, "Lew placed all confidence in the Sydney doctor who had been treating him. The doctor found Lew's spinal discs had not been displaced, but that a ligament beside them was stretched.

"He placed him in a plaster cast, gave him special exercises and gradually cured him."

It was this statement by Mrs. Hoad that provided me with an insight into the character of the youth I would face during 1958—a young fighter who refused to give up even after doctors had read his requiem.

Trying to familiarize myself with Lew, I began assimilating scraps of information I had heard about him, adding to my own personal observations. I recalled that he didn't give a damn about diet, once stating, "I'm fond of ice cream and bananas for breakfast, so why shouldn't I eat them?"

I could hardly conceal a laugh at this, recalling that I was a beans and Coca-Cola man myself. But one man who wouldn't think it funny was Jack Kramer. If he had his way —and he generally does—Lew's diet, especially the early morning one, would change to the more conventional breakfast type.

Lew had little formal instruction. At nineteen he was already an Australian hero, having beaten the ears off the Americans challenging for Davis Cup honors. He wore his hero's mantle unconcernedly. "I won," would be his only comment after taking a big match. If he lost he would explain with equal feeling, "I lost," letting it go at that, minus excuses. And for a losing tennis player to be fresh out of excuses is heresy.

Under the globe-circling taskmaster, Harry Hopman, boss of the Aussie Davis Cup team, Lew was a revolutionary —hating rules and regimentation. Failure to do roadwork, using the wrong knife or fork, or profanity was punishable by small fines in the Hopman camp. Lew was steadfastly guilty of these offenses, regularly paying a shilling here or there. Some have said that Hopman himself absorbed the fines.

Hoad is a cool customer before a tremendously important match. He displays no emotions. His eyes are dreamy, his manner carefree.

Quoting from *Life* magazine, "One day his casualness

caused a minor panic. One of his teammates explains, 'The
Duke and the Queen were there and we were all a bit jumpy,
you know. When it was time for the match we suddenly
couldn't find Lew. We looked all over the place and finally
there he was, fast asleep on the massage table.' "

See what I mean?

Physically, Lew is a fine specimen. Accent is on the wrist.
He attacks on backhand as well as forehand. His service is
something discharged from a cannon. Opponents may beat
him, but they'll never tire him out. He rarely breathes hard,
and between sets, when most exhausted players drop gratefully into a chair for a few moments of precious rest, Lew, of
course, follows the custom. Yet it seems he would prefer standing or starting right in again.

In summation, Lew may be a tough nut for Kramer to
crack and orient into the pro game where you have to put out
100 per cent every match. When an Aussie plays Davis Cup
for the honor of his country, he's a fighting terror. When
playing for cash, there could be just the slightest let-down.
This is pure speculation on my part. Lew's wife, Jennifer,
may help. Jennifer herself is a member of the Australian
women's team. If Kramer wins her over to his side, she may
be able to help shape her husband's moods.

In the pro game, Lew must learn how to pace himself.
This phase of the game took me years to conquer. You just
don't blast every first service. You learn to place the ball,
change tactics and become tricky. Amateurs, even if the score
is love-40 against them on their opponent's serve, go all out
for the point. Not so the pros. Only if the score is deuce or
to their advantage do they make a herculean effort for a service break. Lew is a spectacular shot-maker, a specialist in the
put-away and crosscourt placement. He'll have to curb these
temptations in the professional ranks, eliminating chances of
erring.

State College
9 Double

1 uncle Hawk

DIARY OR JOURNAL
MEMORANDA (ABOVE)

Lew admitted he expected it to be tough as a pro, stressing, "You can't miss the easy shots and win." How right he is. No pro can afford to blow a setup, just like a golf pro can't flub a short putt. Lew acknowledges he has lots to learn. Every freshman pro does.

While the plans for our tour were being made someone asked Lew how he expected to fare against me. "I think I have a better opportunity than anybody else," he said. "After all, I will have had a six months' period to get ready for him. Maybe Pancho will get soft. He's almost thirty now. At that age it's tough to take a layoff and then come snapping back."

Pro debut for Lew came in Jack Kramer's 1957 Tournament of Champions at the West Side Tennis Club, Forest Hills. Lew took Frank Sedgman apart, 6-3, 6-4, 6-4. Newspapers heralded the feat as a "smashing success." They were a bit premature. Sedgman, who moves with the agility of a cat, had been out of competition for over a year and his game was a far cry from its former sharpness. No one can take a long layoff and hope for anything but mistiming.

The tournament was a round-robin affair in both singles and doubles, and offered ten-thousand-dollar prize money. Competing were the leading six pros in the world: Hoad, Sedgman, Rosewall, Segura, Trabert, and myself. I bowled over Rosewall, 6-2, 8-6, 6-4; Sedgman, 5-7, 7-5, 3-6, 6-3, 6-3; Trabert, 6-3, 3-6, 11-9, 6-3; Segura, 6-4, 6-3, 6-4, and was ready for the final-day match against Hoad.

But Hoad on that hot blistering day wasn't ready for me. I won 9-7, 6-4, 3-6, 6-3 and felt that I was always in command. Lew's chief fault was trying to finish a shot before it was really completed. He got out of position too fast. After the execution, he sped for the center of the court too rapidly. His overhead drew raves. If I lofted one to him the best thing for me to do was to seek cover under the umpire's stand.

He used the same grip as Frank Sedgman. If anybody

anywhere has any similarity whatsoever to Frank Sedgman, that's enough to place me on my guard. I would unhesitatingly place Frank as second in the world rankings.

Lew showed he is basically an offensive player. He can't change pace yet, and this hurts his game. It's bang, bang, bang all the way, and when those sizzling shots develop in accuracy I'm in for plenty of trouble.

Where I was surprised was on my service. I thought I could back Lew up a few feet. I couldn't. He stood just inside the baseline waiting stoically for anything I sent his way. Only Segura stands so close on me.

After a nine-day run, here's the final singles standing in the Tournament of Champions:

	W	L
Gonzales	5	0
Sedgman	3	2
Hoad	2	3
Trabert	2	3
Rosewall	2	3
Segura	1	4

Trabert and Sedgman proved too powerful a duo during the doubles competition, snaring first place. Rosewall and I took second. Then it was on to Los Angeles, for a replay, called this time the Master's Tournament. Dinny Pails was added to the cast, and all matches were to be two out of three sets.

While Jack had anticipated a splendid turn-out for this tournament—its second year—he must have received one of the pleasantest surprises of his life when the fans fought to buy tickets. Myron McNamara, publicity director of World Tennis, Inc., who would part with a free ducat as readily as his right leg, performed in his customary manner by handing out few passes. I spent three hundred dollars on tickets for friends.

At the conclusion of the firing I had won another one and was some three thousand dollars richer. I dropped one match, a thriller to Ken Rosewall, 22-20, 1-6, 6-2. Then Trabert and Sedgman obliged by eking out wins over Ken. Sedgman, against whom I'm always at my best, was the man I had to beat on the final afternoon. Entering the contest a 3-1 clubhouse favorite, I won 6-1, 3-6, 6-1. Hoad was easy for me, and everybody picked on him. Again Rosewall and I grabbed second place in the doubles behind Trabert and Sedgman.

Against Frank, I won the match early in the third set. All that's needed in this pro business is one quick break and the handwriting is on the wall. Three backhand passing shots that angled cross-court wrapped it up for me, breaking Frank's serve. After that I simply held my own and I was home.

Lew proved a bitter disappointment. One reporter wrote, "He played like an amateur." I wouldn't go so far as to belittle him that much. I would say that he simply didn't look like a $125,000 investment, after losing every match.

The money I won in this and the Forest Hills tournament averaged in excess of three hundred dollars per day; not bad for work that is enjoyable. I can only guess at the Los Angeles tournament gross, but I'd put it at better than fifty thousand dollars.

The usual number of stars from the entertainment world were present. I noticed Dick Powell, June Allyson, Walter Pidgeon, Doris Day, Ginger Rogers, Rita Hayworth, Howard Duff, Mark Stevens, Groucho Marx, MacDonald Carey, Burt Lancaster, and there were dozens more I couldn't identify with the lights in my eyes.

Friends of Sedgman had hinted of his having bursitis in his arm, combined with a bad leg muscle. Frank waved aside any alibis. "Pancho just beat me," he said. "I felt fine, fine as can be expected at the end of a long tournament like this. I think Pancho has changed his game. He used to try power-passing shots. Now he passes you with sharp angles and dink shots."

I can't agree with Frank's theories concerning changing my game. True, I changed my style against him, but against others I'd play my old tactics. I felt that to hit the ball hard to Frank would only be leaving myself open for errors. When he's knocking off those volleys, he is unbeatable. I'd rather try moving him around since I knew he was pretty tired. I've been lucky against him. One of these days that guy is going to handle me.

16 My Feud with Jack Kramer

Once I fought in a big war against dictatorship, and now I'm doing it again. Only this time the fight doesn't involve so many people. It's just a private war between promoter Jack Kramer of World Tennis, Inc., me and a piece of paper known as a contract. My signature is on the contract.

Throughout Jack's reign as King of the Pros and his successful tours against Bobby Riggs, Frank Sedgman and myself, Big Jake received a 30 per cent guarantee of the gross. Since those days, to my knowledge, there's been no decline in the price indexes of any commodity on the market from tennis players to a loaf of bread. Everything's gone up. Well, everything but my percentage. That's gone down.

Fresh out of the amateur ranks, I got 30 per cent when Jack walloped me on tour. Hitting the comeback trail a number of years later against Tony Trabert, my share was a flat fifteen thousand dollars. Jack gave me 20 per cent against Ken Rosewall, a figure that later was upped to 25 per cent and called a bonus.

Now my next opponent, Lew Hoad, was signed for a guarantee of $125,000 matched against 20 per cent gross over a two-year period. The sum involved is fifty thousand more than has ever been offered in a pro contract before.

I asked Jack for 30 per cent of the Hoad tour. His answer was "20 per cent." Finally I tried to arbitrate and agreed to settle for 25 per cent, to which Jack still said no.

My feeling is that no professional champion in any sport should earn less than the promoter. Kramer's cut is 50 per cent of the gross in the United States, 55 per cent if the tour goes over three hundred thousand dollars. But on European tours, he divides 75 per cent between the players and Fred Perry, European representative, and takes care of operating expenses out of the 25 per cent left.

Jack has a counter argument. "I made only twenty-seven thousand dollars last year," he claims, and offers to throw open his books to me.

I don't read many books.

Why, I ask myself, my friends and my lawyer, Lou Warren, should I drop in percentages? Have I dropped in class? Can't I make as many, if not more, service aces, placements, and smashes? I'm an improved player and a bigger gate attraction than ever. During the Rosewall tour spectators in large cities like New York, Chicago, Los Angeles, Cleveland, Washington, Boston, and Philadelphia increased around 30 per cent. A lot more people are becoming tennis conscious, and I believe I'm responsible for the trend. I even get a batch of daily fan mail. And a woman in Peoria has named her dog Pancho.

Jack says his reason for holding me down to 20 per cent

is that he's committed to the other players. Fine. I want to see the supporting cast on the tours well paid. They're my friends. They deserve it. But I deserve it also. I can beat anyone in the world, but I'm not being paid in proportion to my ability.

Tennis seems to be the only sport where the champion must take short pay, while the challenger commands fantastic figures. Somebody will have to explain the reason to me. In my book it doesn't figure. I played and defeated Ken Rosewall 51 matches to 26, and had plenty of anxious moments during my matches with the gutty little Aussie. He's a bulldog that's hard to shake off. I played the series with a cyst in my right hand and later picked up a bad case of athlete's foot —perhaps a combination of assorted germs from seventy-seven locker rooms. I still have it.

You never know what ailments are going to strike as the tour stretches into thousands of miles of travel. Anything can happen. Your arches may start hurting in Kansas City; in Detroit you may catch cold; in Reno you may sprain your hand pulling the crank of a slot machine. A tour calls for total abstinence from anything in the slightest way detrimental to fine physical condition.

The position of a pro champ is extremely precarious; something similar to walking a tightrope between two skyscrapers. Lose one tour and you're finished. Then your income can dwindle to the point that you can make out the tax forms yourself without outside assistance. Oh, you can pick up a little change playing the U. S. National Professional Championship at Cleveland, or the World's Professional Championship at Wembley Stadium, London, and perhaps in a supporting role on the tours—but your earning powers have been decimated. You're an also-ran. You become a man with a racket in something that isn't a lucrative "racket" any

longer. So in this business you have to get it while the getting
is good, and there are altogether too few years in which to
pick the frosting off the cake.

I'm thirty years old. To persons middle-aged or old, I'm
still an infant. In tennis, I'm considered close to the wheel-
chair. In this run-run-run vocation when you pass thirty the
reflexes can slow, the legs fail to obey the will of the brain.
I believe I'll be top dog until I'm thirty-five, but who knows
what ambitious, hungry amateur will come to the fore within
the next five years and run my shorts off.

When Jack Kramer added his former doubles partner and
my constant court nemesis, Ted Schroeder, to his World
Tennis, Inc. organization, it came as a surprise to me. Ted
had spent ten years in the refrigeration business, giving it
all up to return to his first love, tennis.

He joins a tightly-knit little group that includes, besides
Czar Kramer, Myron McNamara, publicity; Olin Parks, tour
director; John Stinson, equipment manager; Bob Barnes,
Australian representative; Fred Perry, European representative, and Cecile Kay, secretary.

Ted will work on the booking end of the tours. He's
a quiet fellow who will have to talk much more than he did
while making a splash in tennis circles. Then his flashing
racket did the talking for him, plus the umpire's final words:
"Game and match to Mr. Schroeder."

Bob Falkenburg once made what I considered a choice
remark about Ted during a tournament. Bob said, "Ted's
my doubles' partner, and the only time he's spoken to me in
five days was when he asked, 'Whose serve is it?' "

Ted acts as sort of a liaison man and a patcher-upper of my
troubles stemming from Jack. I like him. He doesn't argue
that I'm wrong, and he doesn't say that I'm right. But, he listens. You can't get mad at a guy who just smokes his pipe,
nods and listens.

My present contract with Jack, signed in December, 1955, runs until December, 1960. That's a long time to be in bondage. It didn't take Lincoln that long to free the slaves.

Of course this hassle places my relationship with Jack on the frosty side. Anything I do with him from now on is purely business. When Jack gave me a 5 per cent bonus against Rosewall he called it an increase in pay. This is a misnomer. A bonus is something given as an incentive or reward. I'd like Jack to take a lie detector test on this point, but I guess such procedure is unheard of in a civil case.

Recently I heard someone remark, "Jack and Pancho need each other." Truer words were never spoken. Jack needs me and I need Jack. He's the promoter and I'm the star—the star who doesn't twinkle very brightly financially. Together we can make money. Divided, we fall on our respective noses. Summing it up, the relationship is comparable to a marriage of convenience with mutual admiration entirely lacking.

I was bitterly opposed to Jack's move when he signed Lew Hoad before the U. S. Nationals and Davis Cup play. So was the Australian Lawn Tennis Association. Jack tossed him into the Tournament of Champions at the West Side Tennis Club, and a replay of the same at Los Angeles, being known there as the Masters' Round-Robin Tournament. Jack's eyes were on the turnstiles, and he knew that Lew would play a tune on the cash register.

My eyes were on the future, and I strongly contended that the Hoad defeats would take the edge off our 1958 one hundred-match tour. It's a matter of record that Lew was badly mangled by my fellow pros. He was as green as a St. Patrick's Day parader's necktie. He lacked confidence.

Jack's argument was, "We're seasoning him." It was the same as a baseball team having spring training. Before meeting me, Lew, playing in various foreign countries, would have had seventy to eighty matches under his belt.

I even tried to help him. I never tried to help an opponent before. Perhaps I'm getting mellow. But in Lew I saw a replica of myself just starting in with the pros and losing night after night. The image softened me.

Yet I still say that even with this seasoning Lew's past performances are bound to bruise the gate.

Yes, this is just one of my multiple disagreements with Jack Kramer. We've had several rows over the use of unauthorized endorsements, but I won't go into that. I'm a big boy now, and I don't like being pushed around, squeezed contractually or taken general advantage of. I'm caught in a wringer and I want out. I'm the best tennis player in the world, and I desire monetary as well as press recognition of this fact.

Speaking of press recognition, it took me years to build up to the level where the public recognized me as the champion. On the Trabert tour the pretty printed poster screamed in large type: JACK KRAMER PRESENTS, and then I followed in small lettering. Half of the audiences still thought Jack was the No. 1 tennis boy in the world.

I threatened to back out of the two round-robin tournaments, but each time Lou Warren and his partner, Eugene Glushon, broke down my resistance. I'm really a pretty peaceful guy who likes to go around petting my boxer dogs, but when I think of how Jack is clamping me down, I begin to breathe fire. He makes like he's doing me a favor when he offers me the same percentage he did against Ken Rosewall and no bonus.

So I went to court in Los Angeles to prove my point. Jack beat me again. The judge ruled I didn't have a case. But I'm hoping for another chance against him. He'll have the first serve, but if he doesn't ace me, LOOK OUT!

Nearly every reporter who interviews me wants to know

of my future plans. I never thought anything in the future was certain except dying. Certainly I've given some thought to what comes after Lew Hoad. Still I hate to look ahead of Hoad. He's my immediate future.

Seriously, I hope to go on knocking off amateur threats for at least five more years, provided there actually exists an amateur threat. Tennis tournaments may well lose their sponsors unless a player of exceptional caliber comes to the fore. Why, in the 1957 Nationals the gallery was so conspicuous by its absence that when a small child began to cry somewhere in the depths of the stadium, it was so noticeable the referee admonished:

"Try to keep that baby a bit quiet, please!"

Some years ago fifty babies could have howled in chorus and I doubt if the noise would have bothered anyone.

I'd also like to see a movie made on my life, and I could either play a role in it or hang around as technical adviser. I believe it would be an inspiration to underprivileged kids. Actor Charlton Heston, a tennis devotee, has shown some interest in my life story and, believe me, any guy who can come down off Mt. Sinai as Moses in *The Ten Commandments* to the tennis courts to play Pancho Gonzales must be one hell of an actor. I've heard that few sports pictures make money, but my life would have a guaranteed Spanish-speaking audience.

By the time I retire from active tennis I hope to have some income property. If any of the tenants play tennis, they'll have an easy time stalling me for the rent.

Where will you teach? I'm asked. I don't think I will. How can I teach when I've never had a single lesson? When you teach you have to keep hitting the balls to your pupils or they'll become discouraged. I doubt if I could do this. I'd be tempted to scorch one down the sidelines.

Anyway, Southern California has enough tennis teachers. Competent instructors like Carl Earn, Harvey Snodgrass,

Bob Harmon, Bob Rogers, Sam Match, Johnny Lamb, Walter Westbrook, Phil Greens, Ray Casey, Vini Rurac, Frank Feltrop, George Toley, Loring Fiske, Jerry Hover and many others.

Tennis has been good to me. It's improved my life. I just moved into a nice red two-story house in a quiet district in South Los Angeles. I gave my old house to my brother, Ralph. He helped me a lot on tours. My boys haven't been sick a day in their lives, and we've always been able to give them good food to eat. I don't know how long this financial independence will last, but it looks promising. I love and respect my mother and my father, and I want to make up for the bad times I gave them as a boy, when I wouldn't go to school.

Speaking of boys, kids look up to me, and young boys need help. Pancho Segura and I have talked a lot about opening a tennis school for kids. I'd like to form a Little League tennis program. My oldest boy is eight now, and he'll be ready for something like that very soon. He thinks and dreams of tennis more than I did at his age. One good example came the time I was going to spank him. "Please, Daddy," he requested, "use a tennis racket instead of your hand."

Young boys need support—just like I did once. When you're of Mexican and Spanish descent very often you don't get off to a good start. It's like running the 100-yard dash and being forced to give a two-yard handicap. The Latin kids and kids from the East Side don't get the promotion they need. They need encouragement. You've got to make tennis available to these kids. That's why we haven't got any good Latin players in Los Angeles.

Tennis is still at a stage where it takes some money to get started the correct way. But you can learn almost as much by watching as by playing. That's what I did. It's tougher, though. Patience is needed. I watched tennis bigshots hit certain shots and tried to duplicate them with old rackets and beat-up balls. By practicing over and over again I licked it.

I hate to think about quitting competitive tennis. I know I'll be forced into retirement some day. But I'd like to stay in sports. I need a challenge for everything I do and sports furnish the challenge. To meet a challenge keeps me interested and alive, sharpening my senses.

Maybe in fifty years I'll slow down to the point where Henrietta will challenge me to a knitting contest. I'll accept. And I'll beat her by ten stitches.

17 The Toughest Tour

I'd enjoy writing off this chapter in a single sentence:

I beat Lew Hoad, 48 matches to 34.

But it's not that simple. Every trick I ever learned, more concentration than was previously required, rigorous conditioning, and, lastly, a maximum of determination were needed before Lew was conquered.

Starting out like a whirlwind he ran up an 8-5 lead in Australia, extended it to 18-9 in this country and I didn't pass him until that night in Kansas City when I went out in front, 22-21. Lew was supposed to roll over and play dead when I lengthened this lead to ten matches. Instead of playing dead he came very much to life, moving to a slim 36-31 deficit and hanging right onto my tail until the wear and tear of the trip sent him to the pits with an aching hip.

At tour's end, back in Los Angeles where I was master in

my own home again (although Henry had just ordered me to take my feet off an end table) I was talking with Larry Negrete, 1957 Public Parks doubles champion who casually mentioned, "It's not that Jack Kramer did anything to you, Pancho, it's what he tried to do."

I knew what Larry inferred. Jack had Lew on the road from the time he turned professional until our first clash in Australia. Lew, together with Jack, Segura, and Rosewall, played all over the world. Lew got slimmer, trimmer, wiser. He was readied for me as no challenger had ever been in the history of professional tennis. It was comparable to the New York Yankees, after a full season of spring training, opening against the White Sox whose squad had just reported for the first game.

Money, I believe, was secondary in Jack's mind when he took Lew on this preliminary tour. The gate would have been just as satisfactory without Lew because many of the countries where they played rarely had a chance to see any stars in action. Jack's motivation was to whip Lew into such fine shape that he would knock me off the throne.

Well . . . he sure came close.

I'm not a mind reader as I have often discovered in poker games with Jack, yet this time I had a piercingly clear picture of what went on inside his head. Lew represented a $125,000 investment and was a genial, easy-to-handle chap. I'm not a genial fellow and, as Jack will tell you, even if you don't ask him, I'm hard as hell to handle. So if Lew beat me all would be rosy for Jack. I'd be out of the pro picture and out of Jack's hair. Lew would be in his rear pocket where he'd peacefully rest, coming out only for money.

I understand that Gar Mulloy, while playing at Wimbledon, used to go to the London Aquarium and stare at fish to relieve tension. Gar's methods may be fine for Gar, but I have different ones. These are not to relieve pressure but to touch off an angry explosion inside which makes me play harder. I don't have to visit an aquarium. I look into a mirror and see the biggest fish in Kramer's special aquarium trapped by a seven-year contract.

When Lew began beating me in Australia and New Zealand the writers had a field day. Almost to a man they deserted Pancho Gonzales, now known as a "sinking ship." "Time has run out on the champion" was the trend of thinking. Out of all the experts and alleged prognosticators only Mercer Beasley supported me.

"Gonzales will win by fifteen matches," he predicted.

The bookies in Australia made Lew a 6-to-5 choice. Improvement of Hoad was cited as the reason, plus my age and lack of incentive. "Pancho is set financially," someone wrote, "and the desire to win will be lacking." How ridiculous this sounded to me! Maybe the writer forgot there's a little unavoidable item in this country called income tax.

This seems a good time to inject a letter written by Gloria Kramer, Jack's wife, to Jeane Hoffman and published in the *Los Angeles Times*.

"Dear Jeane:

Well, you've just got to put this Australia down as the tennis capital of the world! In 10 matches to date 75,000 people have come out, and thousands more turned away. Add 11,000 fans in New Zealand for three matches. And if you want to mention money, the tour has drawn in $135,000 for the 10 matches in Australia and $28,000 in New Zealand.

"No doubt you are surprised that Hoad is leading. So is everybody here. I keep saying to Jack, 'Why is Lew winning?' Because, earlier when Jack had written to me from Europe, he said what a great kid this Hoad was—but he didn't think he'd ever win!

"Obviously, the little 'warmup' trip to Europe under the tutorship of Jack did a lot of good. Also the steady competition against Pancho Segura, Ken Rosewall and Jack. It's sort of cute how Jack watches over Lew like a mother hen. Lew is very well liked by all the boys, at least the ones working for Jack. Wonderful disposition, very co-operative, will do anything to help make this tennis a success.

"I'm not an authority, but from a spectator's view (and not a very good one, at that) Lew appears the stronger. He's built like an ox. Pancho seems to tire quickly. Lew is thinking intelligently, and hitting with tremendous confidence. There have been some fabulous shots by both.

"As for the relationship between Pancho and Lew, all I can say is that Lew has such a great disposition, you can't get mad at him. In the three matches I've seen, Pancho behaved very well, although the first match in Wellington was under a terrible wind, and it bothered Lew so much that Pancho won easily. That was the first match I saw in New Zealand. After that, Lew not only won the next four in Christchurch, Auckland and two in Perth, but all wins were in straight sets.

"Just a minute and I'll ask the boys if anything is wrong with Pancho. That's what people will probably start asking, isn't it?

"No, nothing is wrong with Gonzales that anyone knows about. The regulars at the L. A. Tennis Club will have a lot to talk about figuring this one out. Incidentally, when the boys go into America for the opening in San Francisco I think the score will be 8 to 5, because the single matches will soon wind up down here.

Love

Gloria."

Gloria expressed the situation pretty well. No, there was nothing basically wrong with me that a tour grind wouldn't fix up. Hoad is very strong and he is built like an ox and if I wanted to make a bad joke I'd say that I love to eat oxtail soup. And speaking of soup and cooking in general, Lew wasn't going to get any more of a native Australian speciality which was kangaroo tail soup. He was about to embark on a foreign diet. I knew what my stomach was made from—cast

iron. Lew's stomach was going to get severely tested from
restaurant to restaurant, night after night, and the strain of
the eyes—whether he's driving or a passenger—watching that
concrete ribbon of roadway could exact its toll.

To get down to the main reason why we play—money—
the tour, the National Professional Championship which I
copped in Cleveland, the Masters that I won at Forest Hills,
the Masters that I didn't win in Los Angeles, foreign exhibitions and endorsements netted me around ninety-one thousand dollars during the playing year, 1957-58. Now I know
that all you office slaves clerking and filing away at seventy-
five dollars per week will think this over and come up with,
"How can he be mad at Jack Kramer when he earned that
nice chunk of dough?"

Well, I can. I'm not going to rehash why. I did that earlier
in the book.

Melvin Durslag, sports columnist on the *Los Angeles
Examiner,* asked Jack if I had any nice qualities.

The answer was:

"I hate to admit it, but he does. For one thing, he's very
good-hearted. He's also a very determined player. He's
loaded with guts. He's very trusting. He has never yet asked
to look at my books. And he's also honest. I would leave all
the money I own in an open locker next to his and feel confident he'd never take a penny."

Thanks, Jack. I'm not going to pass along my opinion of
you. I'm not a hypocrite.

Jack also mentioned to Durslag that if "Pancho ever got
me over a barrel, he's going to turn the crank."

There's no opportunity for a barrel or a crank in that iron-
clad contract which has my signature at the bottom. I've committed seven years of my life to him and even if he has put
money into my pockets I've earned it the hard way under a

trying condition. Did you ever hear of anyone in the Army loving his sergeant?

The Hoad tour was the worst strain I ever went through. Frankly, I'm not too anxious to play him again. Even when my lead widened I couldn't afford to relax. I'd replay every match in my mind hours after it was over. Especially those I lost. I'd be mean for days, even scowling at waitresses and strangers on the street. A scowl didn't have much effect on Lew. It's hard to see across the court.

March was the great month of the tour for me. I began to regain my touch, move in and handle Lew's second service better and I dropped down to my normal playing weight. A friend said, "Pancho, you're a cinch to win the athlete of the month award."

"I doubt it," I growled.

"Wait and see."

I waited. I saw. They gave it to Silky Sullivan. Silky Sullivan, in case your memory needs jogging, is a horse.

On the tour I drove a Thunderbird. Alone. Those nights I lost and traveled to another city I really took it out on that car, in the form of abuse. And then I'd tinker it back into shape again. Tinkering with a car is the best therapy I know of. I found out that I average nearly 20 miles per hour faster on nights that I lose.

Professional tennis strains a person more than any other sport. In basketball, football, or baseball when a player is hurt a substitute jumps in. This never happens in tennis. You've got to go on nearly every night. I've played with a sprained ankle and Lew splattered himself against a wall that nearly jarred his teeth loose, but finished out the match. Blisters, calluses, cramps, etc., are occupational troubles too minor to even mention.

During the mornings when time hangs heavy on our hands

some of the boys visit museums to sop up culture. I never do. Maybe this is regrettable. I'm certainly not proud of it. The truth is that I just don't get any kick from cultural pursuits. All I want to do is bang the ball where my opponent isn't. When I do, a symphony concert or standing in contemplation before the Mona Lisa can't thrill me nearly as much.

We gave the crowds—crowds that broke all records to see us—some pretty good matches. Since a tennis player never forgets I can recall that the real crowd-pleasers were in White Plains, New York, San Francisco, Los Angeles, Cincinnati, Louisville, Kansas City, Missouri, Memphis, and St. Louis. There were also a share of bad ones. They were in Madison Square Garden, River Oaks, Muncie, Indiana, Toledo and Tampa, Florida. On these nights nothing worked for either of us.

When Lew's hip began bothering him, Jack flew his own personal doctor, Omar Fareed, from Los Angeles to take care of him. Dr. Fareed had previously done a good job with the cyst on my racket hand. At his suggestion, Lew dropped out of the tour in May. The play stoppage cost him somewhere between twenty-five hundred and four thousand dollars. On several occasions during the tour Hoad had twinges of pain. Tests at the UCLA Medical Center confirmed the original diagnosis of Dr. Fareed that Lew was hobbled by right sciatic neuritis. It is believed this condition was an outgrowth of Hoad's previous back trouble. Physical therapy and drugs were prescribed.

Early on the tour when I swung into stride taking sixteen of twenty-one matches, I was certain Lew would begin to crack and I would win in a breeze. Yet he managed to hang on like a bulldog. After I had a 10-point bulge, 33 to 23, he thumped me in East Orange, New Jersey, and went on to win the next four times. You see what I mean? I hope that I never meet a finer competitor. He really gave it all he had. Two of our matches will long remain in my memory. At Kooyong Stadium, Melbourne, Lew slid by me 4-6, 9-7, 11-9, 18-16. The struggle lasted three hours and forty-five minutes. Another marathon occurred in the Masters at Los Angeles. This time I downed him, 3-6, 24-22, 6-1.

I want to touch a bit upon Perry T. Jones' appointment to captaincy of the United States Davis Cup team. It's a well-deserved honor, arriving at long last to a man who has devoted his life to fostering tennis. He's been in the promotional end of the game for forty years. Before then, he was a fine player.

All Mr. Jones needs is one great player and we'll regain the Cup. He'll get that player, but when and who it will be, I'm not certain. The pros have worked with Barry McKay, and it might be big Barry; or even Chris Crawford, a Northern California youth; perhaps young Earl Buckholz is only a few years away. Southern Californians have high hopes for Don Kierbow. Little is known of Don except that in one of his recent brief tournament appearances he ousted Herbie Flam. And reaching far into the younger generation don't count my son Richard out of things, if you'll pardon the parental prejudice.

What amateurs are coming up for serious professional consideration? By "serious" I mean to play the role of challenger and not a member of the supporting cast. Only two: Ashley Cooper and Mal Anderson, both of Australia. Cooper bagged a rare "triple" in 1958—the Australian, Wimbledon, and U. S. crowns. Only the French Championships eluded him. At the present time I don't think he's ready to extend me, but if Jack ever signs him or Mal and benefits them by a slow seasoning and ripening process, I might have my troubles. Both are the phlegmatic type, schooled in the Harry Hopkins

drawing room etiquette manner of gentlemanly tennis players. These boys are hard to ruffle and never let off steam on
the courts.

I got a big kick and a loud laugh the day Kramer amplified
his feelings about me before the press at Forest Hills. "I'd
like to get out from under this burden," he said, referring to
me as the burden. "I am fed up with Pancho's gripes, his
constant demands and his repeated holdouts. I can't find out
what he wants. I can't make schedules or commitments. I told
Pancho just this week that he could buy the contract himself
if he wanted it at a reasonable price."

Jack called fifty thousand dollars a reasonable price.

Of course this idea wasn't original. Slaves bought themselves out of bondage thousands of years ago. The world
hasn't changed much. Only the prices.

Sure, Jack's willing to sell my contract. He knows he hasn't
got an outstanding amateur to play me next year. He's desperate. If there was a good amateur or pro coming along,
Jack wouldn't think of selling.

Well, be it Cooper or Anderson or Lew Hoad again in the
near future, you can be sure of one thing—I'll show up. Every
year from now on the critics will refer to my "slowing down"
and be watchful for indications of decay. Their typewriters
and words from mouths will be trying to make an old man
out of me before my time.

The rocking chair's a long way off.

I'm the best damned tennis player in the whole wide world
and I expect to remain so for a long, long time.

Bring on the challengers, Jack!

This book requires an appendage.

*It is necessary so that the readers won't construe the emo-
tions exhibited by Henry and me toward each other as tinged
with hypocrisy. Our feelings are unchanged since the day we*

married. *I love her; and I believe she loves me. Only we can't
live together any more.*

Henry and I are divorced.

*On December 22, 1958 in the Los Angeles Domestic Rela-
tions Court before Superior Judge Burnett Wolfson, an
agreement was consummated to the mutual satisfaction of
both parties.*

*When I use the word "satisfaction" I mean monetarily
speaking. The heart has been excluded.*

*I understand Henry's attitude. She says that I haven't
matured enough to accept my responsibilities in life. She is
referring to herself and the three boys.*

*Maybe she's right. But I think it goes deeper than that.
Perhaps I have some psychoneurosis. I just can't hold still
long enough to be a model husband. I can't relax. I've got
too much energy. I can't come home at night, put on my
house slippers and lead a domestic, by-the-fireside existence.*

*In this book I have the last word and by using this preroga-
tive to speak of our breakup, I am in no way seeking sympathy. A long time ago I came to the conclusion that I'm not
composed of the stuff good husbands are made of.*

*Something inside makes me want to run, run, run—in all
directions—and none of them lead toward my home.*

18 Tips for Beginners

Obviously, the most important thing in tennis is the racket; without one, the game cannot be played. Thus it stands to reason that after purchasing a racket this instrument of pleasure should be afforded choice treatment. Tape the end of the frame if you're scraping cement courts, place in a press after using, slip into a case, clip any frayed strings, shellac when necessary. Don't be afraid to coddle it like a baby.

Above all, don't buy a cheap racket. A cheap racket is comparable to a cheap fishing rod. In the case of the latter, a cast can't quite make it where the big one is splashing; in tennis, a shot will be missed that normally could be made if the racket is first-class.

A price-conscious mother whose son intends learning the game may argue, "We can't afford an expensive one. We'll start him out with a cheap one and then get him a better one later on." This is just another penny-wise and pound-foolish argument. If you follow this line of thinking, you will invariably end up buying two rackets instead of one.

Rackets—by arrangement with tennis shop proprietors— may be bought on time payments. Look upon this expenditure as not just a purchase of wood and tightly drawn and laced strings, but as a long-term annuity policy guaranteeing fine physical condition, socializing, and sportsmanship.

Getting down to fundamentals.

FOREHAND. Tennis grips come in three choices. Forget any of the modifications or exaggerations you may hear about, such as my own hammer grip. For the forehand, use the Eastern grip. The Eastern grip is obtained by shaking hands with the racket much in the manner you would shake hands with a friend.

On the forehand, you either draw the racket back straight or take a circular swing. No two forehands are exactly alike. They vary like fingerprints. The circular swing leads the field in popularity and is the ultimate in rhythm. Hit the ball flatly with a good follow-through. No turn of the racket. No hitting up motion. Forget topspin. Topspin slows speed, enabling opponents to cover the shot easier while a well-hit flat shot fairly flies toward the backstops.

Extend your left foot toward the net but don't point the toe. On every return that isn't high the knees must be bent, if possible. Stand like a ramrod and you'll never be a tennis player. At first, knee bending is difficult. Soon it becomes an automatic reflex.

Hold the racket tightly. Keep a stiff wrist. A loose, floppy wrist is the curse of tennis.

Most instructors from time to time bellow: "Keep your eye on the ball!" I never stress the point. The eye can't be blamed for an error. I assume the pupil is going to keep his eye on the ball by sheer instinct. It's almost self-protective: keep your eye on the ball and hit it or it will hit you. Naturally, a space judgment is necessary to quickly and accurately measure your distance from the ball. This also develops through instinct.

BACKHAND. The backhand frightens many beginners. They hate to take a shot on what they feel is the wrong or weak side. True, you can't hit the backhand with the speed of the forehand for as many placements, but you can develop it to the point of less errors. It can easily become the steady, always dependable side of your game.

Shots to the backhand cause the beginner to develop a tendency to run around balls in order to get off a forehand shot. Of course some running is acceptable where the chance for an unreturnable shot is presented. Otherwise don't consider any running around the backhand. Valuable time is given your opponent on such maneuvers.

For a backhand grip the racket must be turned slightly, the top rim moving a couple of inches toward the right. Never put your thumb straight up; lay it across the handle. In this position, the backhand can be driven in the manner of the forehand or hit for safety's sake with a little underspin. Watch the head of your racket. If it drops, it's a danger sign. Keep it up, above the wrist level.

SERVICE. To be able to serve you must possess a strong, agile back that is pliable and can be bent and twisted. Sufferers from sacroiliacs, discs, etc., will undergo trouble and ofttimes considerable pain executing the proper services.

The generally accepted beginner's service is a slicing form of delivery abetted by the Continental grip. Hold the racket in your left hand directly in front of you. Grip the racket by the throat. Now, fasten the fingers of your right hand on top of the handle. That's the Continental.

Stand barely behind the baseline, feet spread, weight adjusted in a way that it shifts toward the court after the ball is struck. Never toss the ball in excess of two or three feet over your head. Throw it slightly ahead of yourself above the left shoulder.

Racket and ball meet at the height of the toss for the forward swing. After the racket descends you will find the head of it traveling by the side of your right leg. The serve requires more coordination than any single stroke and infinitely more practice. It is a combination of movements that gradually merge into a continuous one.

Once the simple slice service is mastered, the pupil may advance to the twist by giving his back an arch and throwing the ball so that he has to reach for it over his left shoulder. After this service lands it has spin, often jumping to the opponent's backhand, forcing him out of position.

Additional speed can be generated by a first service variation of this twist by tossing the ball up over your right shoulder and hitting it with the full face of the racket. Although this move eliminates spin, exceptional speed is gained with the chance of service aces being scored.

THE VOLLEY. No grip changes are necessary in going from the Continental grip service to the volley. Learning to volley (hitting the ball while it comes toward you in the air) is a step that is in comparison to graduating from high school to college. Here the beginner shakes off his apprenticeship, advancing to the stage where he can furnish anybody with a good singles workout and be desirable as a fourth for doubles. Nearly any player can learn to hit a fair ball from the baseline, but to move netwards and hit the ball while in flight is a different matter.

The majority of learners rush forward to crowd the net instead of standing the most advantageous distance from it, which is halfway between the net and the service line. The pupil's knees should be slightly bent. The backswing is short; the shorter the better, with elbow bent. Don't wait until the ball is opposite you; hit the volley when the ball is well in front and punch at it like a boxer delivering a short jab. It is a short, punching, crispy stroke. Every volley has underspin. Underspin gives you ball control.

THE SMASH. The smash is exactly what the name implies, a crashing overhead stroke with the same grip as the volley and service. It always reminds me of an anti-aircraft gun downing a plane. Anything in the air you hit and hit hard, shifting weight to unload all possible power into the stroke. A clean smash can provide a great, uplifted feeling—the feeling of sheer power.

Not every overhead, of course, can be smashed. On some you may be out of position, or backing up. On these you must settle for half-power.

Never allow an overhead to bounce if you can hit it safely in the air. Your opponent may be out of position and scurrying toward the center of the baseline. If you let the ball bounce first, you give him time to get into position and anticipate your shot.

DON'TS FOR THE BEGINNER

Don't foot fault. That white line has not been placed where it is by some brush-happy painter or whitewasher. It's a boundary. Observe it.

Don't return service using a half stroke. Whenever possible use a full swing.

Don't play with balls until they are worn down to the skins. A light ball floats, the wind plays havoc with it, and the loss of weight from missing nap takes the real pleasure out of stroking.

Don't try a running, driving, forehand volley. This is far too difficult for the beginner to master.

Don't try to shave the sidelines or nick the baseline with drives. Keep hitting well inside the court.

Don't try to drive the ball at your opponent while he is at the net.

Don't try low lobs until you've reached an advance stage of the game. A poorly hit low lob sets up a "cripple" for your opponent.

Don't purposely attempt half-volleys, which means hitting the ball on pickups. A half-volley is often a desperate save and almost always purely defensive.

Don't try hitting balls on the rise. Hit them at the crest of the rise. Only the very talented can hit on the rise.

Don't lose concentration. Rid your mind of everything except the game you are playing.

Don't keep hitting to your opponent. Keep moving him at all times.

Don't present an unkempt appearance. Tournament and club officials want to see a neat player with an all-white appearance.

Don't take too long to serve. Your opponent may do the same thing to you.

Don't attempt to barely clear the net on drives. Keep a safe distance between the ball and net.

19 Not for Beginners

Just learning to play tennis?

If such be the case, pay no attention whatsoever to the contents of this chapter. Run—do not walk—to a tennis instructor, and discover in slow, graduated stages the rudiments of the game. Begin while you're barely big enough to clutch a racket in your tiny hand. Years later, when the blisters and calluses heal, open the book to this chapter. Perhaps then, and I use the word "perhaps" with many reservations, assimilation can follow.

Let me first speak of condition. Condition is of cardinal importance. It is a state of body, not of mind. Condition alone can win matches. In the fifth set if you're 5 per cent stronger, you can be 25 per cent worse and still win.

Better read the last sentence again . . . slowly. Digest it. Every word screams the truth.

To be in tip-top condition before a match, eat a light meal from two to four hours before the start of play. The more sleep you get, the better. There is no such thing as being over-slept before a match. Each extra hour in bed means extra stamina on the court. Should a little tension exist and inter-fere with sleep, pick a pleasant subject to concentrate on. Never pick your opponent. Think of counting money, think of a pretty girl, think of a beautiful sunset. But no sedatives. Never, never any sedatives.

Manage to wake from sleep at least an hour before match time. Sleeping up to the final few minutes makes it difficult to shake off lethargy. Don't watch TV or go to a movie di-rectly before a match. You'll suffer unconscious eye strain. It's tough enough to focus a pair of rested eyes on a ball, let alone tired ones.

IMPORTANT. Warm up for at least twenty minutes. Should your opponent show an eagerness to get started and keep ask-ing, "Are you ready?", simply keep answering "no." Don't let him hurry you. Don't figure on gradually easing into the match and waiting for an opportunity to spurt into the lead. Start fast! Serve your speediest serve the very first time it's your turn. Get the early jump. The jump can mean the match.

Never lose concentration. Forget the girl who jilted you, income tax, mounting bills. Turn off all stray thoughts.

Keep an even temperament. Players have been known to lose matches when irked by a bad line call. And don't think you won't get plenty of them. Forget petty annoyances like applause at the wrong time and loud voices in the stands. Or even a fly. I've seen a player blow an important match because a fly annoyed him. Remember, that same fly can cross the net and buzz around your opponent. Don't let it bother you if most of the applause is for your competitor. Maybe he has more relatives. As long as he isn't related to the umpire, you're safe.

During intermission time after the third set, lay off hot showers. Take them lukewarm. A few minutes under the water is enough. Under no circumstances drink cold liquids. Cast aside the temptation. Hot tea is good. Lemon-sucking keeps the inside of the mouth just right. A small glass of orange juice is fine for energy restoring. Salt tablets are strongly recommended. Too much liquid is a condition destroyer and slows you down within a few games. Running becomes as difficult as rowing a water-logged boat.

Before meeting an opponent, if possible, study his style. Learn his weak points and, believe me, every player has at least one. Ask other players for advice. They will readily expound their knowledge. No one is impregnable. Hammer at these weaknesses, even if they seem strong points in the beginning. You'll eventually break them down.

Try to be fair at all times. Never quick-serve, or take too much time on the service. If you're fair with your opponent, generally he'll be fair with you. Don't stall. If you're out of gas, stalling won't help much. Only a rainstorm will save you then. Should anything bother you, tell the umpire. He'll try to correct the situation. Don't take it out on the poor innocent ball boys or the linesmen. They're doing you a favor by showing up.

If you're a young player, I'll safely guess that you are trying to hit too hard. Forget blasting. Learn to keep the ball in play. I don't mean by pat-balling but by solid stroking. Forget nicking the sidelines. It would be difficult enough nicking them with a rifle bullet, let alone a tennis ball. Certainly you may score a brilliant unreturnable shot, but you're flaunting percentages. Playing percentages pays off. Above all, eliminate the idea of fantastic crosscourt shots. Learn to send up a

high lob in order to get back into position—a real high deep
one—even if it brings rain.

RUN, RUN, RUN your opponent. A player forced to run to
hit a shot has far less chance returning it than one who doesn't
have to move. Don't give him what I call the "rocking chair
shot."

Going back to lobs, make sure they come down near the
baseline. A short lob is fatal. Keep away from trying to master the low, topped lob. When this lob strikes the court, it
shoots toward the backstop and proves almost unreturnable.
Admittedly one of the brilliant shots of tennis, it's too hard
to learn. The Kinsey brothers were specialists at this, but if
you're not a member of the immediate family, forget it.

Don't even think about a drop shot. They are rapidly becoming a thing of the past. If you're a woman, though, use it.
There is no better weapon for draining an opponent of stamina. The speed of men cuts down its effectiveness. The drop
shot of importance is the drop volley. It requires a sensitive
touch. The payoff is big. Hours of practice will provide you
with one. Don't be discouraged by repeated failures the first
week. Keep practicing.

Change of pace is also outmoded. Years ago it was considered superb strategy when two players stood in the back court
and the ball crossed the net dozens of times. Tilden once engaged in a rally where the ball went over the net 126 times.
Today, if you play the big game, the ball is lucky to travel
back and forth four times in a single point. So change of pace
becomes meaningless when an opponent whacks the ball in
flight. The only change of pace I've observed is the uninten-
tional one of going from bad to lousy.

If you are playing clay, cement, wood, or grass for the first
time, practice on the surface a couple of days in advance. The

difference is tremendous, especially indoors on wood. The long, deeply stroked backhand loses its authority here unless shortened considerably. You'll rarely have to think about any wood except that in your racket frame unless you fill out an entry blank for the National Indoor in New York. The transition from grass to hard court is not easily managed, and the results bring upsets in form. Remember this: the highest bounce is on clay, followed by cement and then grass.

Time to speak of the serve. Periodically cross up your opponent by hitting the second service first. This maneuver gives you more time to storm the net due to the high hop of the ball. It's pretty foolish trying to baffle an opponent by employing your fast first service on the second serve. Again, you're bucking percentages.

Another pointer is on service return. If you return it short and your opponent lowers his head to hit the ball, don't stand in one place. Keep active. Being conscious of the fact that you are running may cause him to take his eye off the ball for a fraction of a second to see where you are. Due to your movements he may overplay the shot. A departure from the conventional on receiving serve is to shift in position toward the backhand as if you believe it is weak and you are protecting it. Thus, when the server sees more court open he will make a flash decision to try for an ace which can cause a fault.

In running for a well-placed lob barely within range, learn to lengthen the grip on your racket, holding it in a stiff-arm position. Extra inches are proved, and a few additional inches may spell the difference in making or erring on the shot.

Dwelling for one paragraph on the racket grip, I cannot fairly advise which one to use, the Western, Eastern, or Continental. Try them all and then do what comes naturally after you have mastered the fundamentals of the game. My own grip has been called by Don Budge and others, a "hammer grip." It is in between the Eastern and Continental, for both forehand and backhand. My fingers are never spread. My hand is at the end of the handle, clutching it like I would a hammer. I wouldn't advise many to copy it. Control is much easier if the fingers are slightly spread.

The weakest link in American tennis has been doubles. Kramer and Schroeder teamed smoothly together, and, of course, there was the famous George Lott and Les Stoefen duo and Johnny Van Ryn and Wilmer Allison, also Don Budge and Gene Mako. After these, memories must be strained to remember outstanding combinations. One reason for our deficiencies stems from too many pickup teams. Continuous changes in team personnel hamper harmonious play. In Australia it is different. There, combinations are enduring. That's why the Aussies have captured 67 per cent of all Davis Cup Challenge Round Doubles matches. Next comes the U. S., with 46 per cent. Doubles is like marriage. Players must know each other's strengths and weaknesses. They must be tolerant. They must encourage and warn during tough sledding.

Chances of a service break in doubles reveal the prohibitive odds of around 7 to 1. For this reason safety measures should be discarded by the team on the receiving end. Everything possible should be done to steal the offensive. Daring play is required.

From the spectator's viewpoint, doubles is more spectacular than singles. It's a slam-bang affair with four players trying to take the net at the same time. However, it is not devoid of light touch shots dumped at the feet of the incoming server, acute angles and lobs.

Many young tennis aspirants say to me, "I can't afford lessons. Have you any suggestions?" Yes, I have. It's the eavesdropping system. Move as close as possible to any court where a teacher is instructing. Keep your eyes and ears open and your feet ready for mercurial duty should the pros chase you away. This is learning the hard way, but you will pick up plenty of pointers. One of our nationally-ranked players used this system.

If you can talk somebody with a home movie camera into shooting pictures of you in action, certain flaws in your game are possible to correct. During screening camera action can be halted precisely when a mistake occurs.

The most truly valuable advice I can offer is never to play against players you can beat. Play those who can beat you. Then you will learn—the hard way, but the productive way. Should your ego require a few victory plums, these can be snatched where they really count most—in tournaments.

Men can learn a lesson from women in that the latter invariably practice against the opposite sex. Once they are used to the harder hitting, there remains little to fear from the comparatively soft shots of members of their own sex.

Never take defeat lightly. It's fine to be a sportsman and smile through your tears while on public display. Surface-wise you can be the carbon copy of a laughing boy, but once exiled from the crowd, brooding should be in order. Deep inside let the loss nettle and goad you into discovering why it happened, and better still, what you are going to do about it should you ever cross rackets again with the same foe.

Try to recall where you made the important mistakes. Practice against a repetition. Practice for hours. Have a rallying partner hit two or three hundred shots to your weaknesses and watch them vanish. Laborious hours must be spent in practice.

Practicing with a tennis machine is a wonderful and modern method for improvement. The machine can be set to send balls to any given place at different speeds. Even lobs. But few have access to such machines. So borrow a human machine—a friend. If you haven't got a friend, find a backboard. Any handball court will do. A backyard fence or the side of a building is next best.

The road leading to the pinnacle of tennis success is bumpy, slippery, steep, lined with pitfalls and booby traps. If you make it, the rewards are incomparable.

I'd sooner be what I am than President.

20 Questions and Answers

Everywhere I go people ask me questions. I try to answer them to the best of my ability. Often it's difficult. I may be hurrying to a match, rushing for a shower, hungry, late for an appointment, or in a bad mood.

To those I gave hasty retorts, I apologize. To those I wouldn't reply, I apologize. To those I gave the wrong answers, I again apologize.

I wish to make amends.

Many of these questions culled from my memory were, I realize, good, honest questions. Some have remained firmly lodged in my mind. Now I am going to answer them.

Q. Do spectators ever bother you?
A. Only by staying away from my matches.
Q. Is amateur tennis in the East snobbish?

A. More so than in the West.

Q. A national magazine once stated you were refused admission into the dining room of the Forest Hills Inn because you weren't wearing a tie. Is it true?

A. No. Some sports writer was reaching for a story.

Q. Do you ever talk jive talk?

A. I don't dig you.

Q. Have you entertained ambitions of becoming a bull fighter? I've heard it mentioned on account of your fast footwork and graceful movements.

A. Never. I like animals too well to stick anything into them but a fork.

Q. If you hadn't become an athlete, what do you think you'd be doing today?

A. Working in a garage as a mechanic.

Q. Do you sleep soundly?

A. Like a dead man. I hear nothing. And I hope no burglars read this.

Q. Would you want your three children to become tennis players?

A. Not champions. Just play a social game.

Q. Could Pancho Segura beat Frank Sedgman on a tour?

A. I don't believe so.

Q. Could Pancho Segura beat Tony Trabert?

A. In any given match, yes. On a tour playing under adverse conditions, I seriously doubt it.

Q. Who's your favorite sports announcer?

A. Sam Balter, KLAC, Hollywood and *Los Angeles Herald-Express* sports columnist. He plays a pretty fair game of tennis himself.

Q. Whom do you hate worse than anyone in the world?

A. I can't think of anybody. People say I'm lazy.

Q. Whom do you consider the best tennis writer in the nation?

A. Allison Danzig, *New York Times.*

Q. Do you believe the national championship will ever be played on hard surface courts?

A. I hardly think so. Grass has tradition behind it even if it does become pretty worn and slippery at times.

Q. Do you believe in lessons?

A. For everyone in the world except myself.

Q. What do you consider the most important stroke in tennis?

A. No doubt, the serve. If you don't believe me ask those considered fairly easy servers like Rosewall, Flam, Segura.

Q. What was the most surprising defeat in your career as both professional and amateur?

A. When as a pro Don Budge beat me on the stage of the Shrine Auditorium, Los Angeles, in my own home town. His tennis was a throwback to his youth.

Q. What's the main difference between pro and amateur tennis?

A. Skill and money. As a pro you earn all your money legitimately.

Q. Do you have any superstitions when you play?

A. Not to my knowledge. I have a habit, however, not far removed from a superstition. When playing I don't roll or fold my socks. I wear them straight up.

Q. Why aren't women tennis players better looking?

A. Did you ever see Gussie Moran, Louise Snow Isaacs, Carol Fageros, Laura Lou Jahn, Nancy Chafee Kiner, and others? But on the whole I'm inclined to agree they aren't exactly starlets. The main reason's sun beating down on them all day. Skin dries up, becomes leathery, legs get muscular, shoulders broader.

Q. Are you romantically inclined?

A. I'm of Latin temperament.

Q. Are you friendly with any movie stars?

A. Yes. Walter Pidgeon, Gilbert Roland, Howard Duff, Doris Day, Ida Lupino.

Q. Any suggestions for recapturing the Davis Cup?

A. Just one. Keep the same men playing doubles together for a number of years.

Q. Give me your definition of a "tennis bum."

A. A tournament player who keeps postponing going to work.

Q. Do your best friends call you Pancho or Dick?

A. Both. Some call me Gorgo. Means gorilla in Spanish.

Q. Are there any amateurs today who could press you?

A. No.

Q. Does your wife accompany you on tours?

A. She'll meet me in certain cities and then fly back home.

Q. What are the best tennis balls to use?

A. I represent A. G. Spalding.

Q. What would be your idea of a super-tennis player?

A. A player with two heads. Then he could intimidate the linesmen and argue with the umpire at the same time.

Q. If a handpicked squad of the best amateurs in the world battled the best pros in a replica of the Davis Cup matches, what would be the outcome?

A. Five to nothing in favor of the pros; with a chance of 4-1. There is a possibility the pros might lose the doubles as they often change partners and rarely play too long as a unit.

Q. Has the drop shot much value in tennis?

A. On a hard surface court, no, except to take a little out of your opponent by running him. On hard surface if you chase the shot you stop short like you have brakes and race into back court for the lob which usually follows. On clay or grass you skid and can't always get back into position in time.

Q. Were you ever socially snubbed or felt you were unacceptable?

A. I wouldn't know. You never find out those things with an ego like mine.

Q. Who is your favorite racket stringer?

A. Arzy Kunz, Olympic Tennis Shop, Beverly Hills, California. Besides mine, he strings Kramer's, Segura's and many other leading players.

Q. Will Mr. Kunz take mail order stringing jobs?

A. He'd be delighted.

Q. Do you advocate showering during the rest period after the third set of a match?

A. In my case, yes. Possibly in the case of a slow starter, no. You can judge what's best for you.

Q. How can you cure "tennis elbow?"

A. You'll have to get medical advice.

Q. What happened to that grand old tradition of leaping the net to congratulate the victor?

A. It probably ended in a flurry of broken legs. It's enough to leap around the court, let alone take a running high jump when you're dog-tired after a match.

Q. If you win the spin of the racket for choice of court or serve, which would you take?

A. The service, even if yours is weak.

Q. Name your favorite tennis book.

A. The one you're reading.

Q. If a tennis ball gets wet, will it become dead?

A. No.

Q. If you had your life to live over again would you make any changes?

A. Only one. I'd never learn to play poker.

Q. Why was Pancho Segura one of the last players to wear shorts?

A. The answer is obvious when you study his legs.

Q. Will smoking injure your game?
A. I've posed in a Viceroy advertisement.
Q. How good is a nylon gut?
A. Lasts a long time and is excellent for beginners, poor for tournament players.
Q. Is there anything that can be done to restore life to a dead tennis ball?
A. Heating them in an oven gives a temporary higher bounce.
Q. Does a windy day bother you?
A. No more than my opponent.
Q. Some people say you'd like to be an actor. Is it true?
A. I'm already one every time I'm on a court.
Q. Do women use drop shots more than men?
A. Yes. It's a deadly weapon made to order for women's play because the other sex can't cover the court as fast. Beverly Baker Fleitz and Dottie Knode are masters of this specialty.
Q. What's the most difficult shot in tennis?
A. The drop volley, which is difficult to execute. They must be just eased over the net, sharply angled. They require a fine touch.
Q. What's the size of your racket handle?
A. Four and three-quarters.
Q. What weight racket does Jack Kramer use?
A. He uses a 15, which is too heavy a war club for me.
Q. Name the advantages of playing on grass over cement.
A. Cooler, kinder on the muscles and more traditional.
Q. What should the beginner learn first?
A. Ground strokes.
Q. After intermission following the third set, is any practice serving allowed?
A. No.
Q. Who were the best lobbers you ever watched?

A. Budge Patty, Ken Rosewall, Tony Trabert, Art Larsen, Maureen Connolly, and Bobby Riggs. Riggs was the best of the lot.

Q. What do you think of two-handed hitting?

A. Twice as difficult to learn as one hand, and not twice as effective.

Q. Where can I sell my used tennis balls?

A. Playballs, 540 South Kenmore, Los Angeles; or American Novelty Company, Box 625, Merrick, L. I., N. Y.

21 Favorite Stories

A good tennis tale always intrigues me, especially an off-beat one that manages to escape from the stereotyped, "I was down 5-0, and match point . . ." kind. There's a scarcity of interesting stories dealing with the sport. The few going the rounds are doled out like half-rations. Players themselves are poor narrators, preferring deeds of the racket to the raconteur. A notable exception is George Lyttelton Rogers, perhaps the tallest big-time competitor in the history of the game.

Rogers, former Irish Amateur Champion, turned pro when he moved to the United States. He still retains his Irish citizenship which gives him the privilege of slight embellishments. This is not intended as a slur on the Irish, and before they swarm down from their green hills demanding a retraction, let me hastily add that I love them.

Returning to George Lyttelton Rogers, the man is a powerful spinner of yarns. He needs no leprechauns, banshees, or
werewolves. His characters are tennis players and in the following story, related to me in London where we faced each
other in a professional tournament, George plays the princi-
pal role. For reading convenience it has been transposed into
the third person.

A CHARACTER FROM IRELAND

When an athlete owns two diverse and outstanding talents,
one must be subjugated. Top-flight success comes only to the
specialist. Such an athlete was George Lyttelton Rogers.

In 1930, Rogers, a gigantic combination of knife-and-forker
and tennis player arrived in the United States to concentrate
on legally lifting some tournament trophies. Had the tour
been confined to restaurants, the depression might have
ended a few years earlier because the visitor could point with
pride and bicarbonate to the following records:

Liquid Department

Drank a magnum of champagne in three minutes flat.

Downed seventeen steins of German beer in thirty minutes.

Tossed off twenty-one straight glasses of water in Paris,
where a single glass of the stuff is considered unusual.

Food Department

Breakfast consisting of five soup bowls of oatmeal, six eggs,
eight slices of bacon, six pieces of toast, washed down with a
full quart of orange juice, topped by three cups of coffee.

Afternoon tea: twenty-one cakes and one cup of tea.

Had the largest single dinner tab in the history of Simp-
sons, famous London roast beef house.

Rogers differed physically from contemporary epicures.

While nourishment bulged the latter's stomachs, the starches, fats, and carbohydrates he consumed ran to length. He was six feet, seven inches tall, thin and wiry.

George Rogers did not come to the United States for the purpose of eating, although it was a habit picked up since he was a baby and one which could not easily be broken. He came here for tennis. While his native Ireland is thought to be the greenest country in the world, he found the United States even greener, the chlorophyll difference fashioned by the coffers of the United States Lawn Tennis Association, where expense accounts, even then, were important issues.

Newspapers immediately tagged the visitor from Erin as the "Irish Giant," and tennis writers with unfailing regularity inserted into their copy "tallest player in the world." He was.

He played a sound all-court game. His towering figure at the net presented lobbing problems. Opponents had to hit, almost high enough skyward to bring precipitation, in order to get the ball over his outstretched arm.

His record was little short of terrific. Naturally, he was the Irish champion, a title he could have won by substituting a shillelagh for a racket. He had swept over the continent like a vacuum cleaner, winning eighteen international tournaments in successive weeks. Henri Cochet, the remarkable little Frenchman, one of the Four Musketeers, and Jack Crawford, the dependable Australian, were among his victims.

Receiving an entry blank from Perry T. Jones, Rogers journeyed to Los Angeles for competition in the Pacific Southwest Tournament at the Los Angeles Tennis Club. This tournament was treated like the Forest Hills of the West Coast. The difference lay in the fact that few, if any, foot faults were called and that during a sensational rally the appearance of a female movie star took spectators' eyes from the flight of the ball to the curves of the torso.

Jones allowed Rogers eighty dollars for round trip food expense from New York to Los Angeles. The train ride was tedious, and there was little to do but wait for the porter's announcement, "The dining car is now open." When Rogers' ears picked up this bit of interesting information, he would disappear down the aisle in a flying welter of arms and legs, hell-bent for the diner.

Upon reaching Los Angeles the first thing the young Irishman did was call on Perry Jones. The conversation went something like this:

"Mr. Jones, my name is George Rogers. Eighty dollars round trip is insufficient expense money for my food."

Mr. Jones was unaccustomed to the direct approach on monetary matters from his players. Usually his well-framed question such as "How are you hitting them?" would derail complaints from money thoughts. Slightly stunned he countered with, "Why not? The average man could eat handsomely on that amount."

"To that I agree," returned Rogers, adding, "but I am not the average man."

"Hmmm," Jones pondered, running his eyes over the elongated Irishman.

While Jones was in such a speculative state of mind, Rogers asked him, "How tall is Bitsy Grant?"

The Atlantan was the smallest of American players ranked in the first ten. Jones knew his tennis statistics. "Five-one" he said.

"Correct," Rogers nodded, and fired another question. "Now how much food money would Bitsy Grant get if he came to this tournament by train?"

"Eighty dollars, same as you," Jones answered without hesitation.

Rogers nodded again and pulled a slip of paper containing neatly inscribed figures from his pocket. Consulting it he read slowly, "Grant is five-one. . . . I am six-seven. Subtracting Grant from me, this leaves a discrepancy of 18 inches."

"But-but. . . ." began Jones.

"So you see," interrupted Rogers, scanning the paper before him, "if little Grant would receive $80 and he's 18 inches shorter than I am, the breakdown is simple. He receives approximately $1.16 per inch. At the additional height advantage I have, or . . ." he paused and glanced sternly at Jones, "don't seem to have in this case, the differential in inches is equal to $20.88.

"Therefore, Mr. Jones, you owe me $20.88."

Jones sighed, helpless against such irrefutable logic and reached for his checkbook. While his fingers wrote, his mind planned to invite Bitsy Grant to the next tournament and use the same figures and logic, but in reverse, on the Georgian.

Rogers drew Lester Stoefen in the first round. Stoefen, a promising junior in those days, was later to become part of a near-perfection doubles duo with George Lott.

The match, played on an outside court, drew hundreds of spectators who were not interested in the fact that the youthful Californian extended Rogers 8-6, 8-6. What attracted them were the shorts worn by the Irishman. Introduced that season by Bunny Austin, the English star, they had failed to capture the fancy of the players after all the years of traditional long white flannels. George Rogers was a progressive. He took to them immediately. They gave him running room. His extraordinarily lengthy limbs resembled hairy undulating poles as they scurried around the court.

At the conclusion of the match Rogers was summoned to Jones' office. The Western tennis major-domo was known as a stickler for conventional court dress.

"Mr. Rogers," he said, "tomorrow you meet Ellsworth Vines in a center court attraction."

"Yes, sir," said Rogers, waiting.

"I want no shorts on the center court," voiced Jones.

Rogers launched a vigorous protest, ending with "I brought only shorts."

Jones had a solution. "Hop into a taxi, buy a pair of flannels and charge them to me." Mentioning the name of the haberdasher he handed over taxi fare.

Rogers was unhappy.

As if to placate him, Jones led him outside where he pointed to the top of the stadium. Here the flags from countries of various competing foreign players blew in the breeze.

"I could locate no Irish flag," Jones said. "But in your honor, when you play tomorrow, there will be one. You have trousers made, I have a flag made. We compromised," he chuckled.

When Rogers arrived at the stadium for his match, he saw, floating from its moorings, a large green flag bearing on the surface a white harp and shamrock. The official Irish flag was blue with a golden harp in the center. He made no comment.

In the locker room, Rogers painstakingly, and not without some torture and the help of a ball boy, managed to work into his new trousers. They bound him severely in the crotch, pressed into his stomach, clutched at his bony knees. He made a test run around the dressing room, listening for ripping sounds. Hearing none, he felt reasonably safe as he went to the court.

In sports parlance when an athlete takes it easy he's "playing under wraps." Well, Rogers didn't take it easy and he was playing under trousers—choking, binding, non-resilient trousers. He was a man with two left feet in two bear traps. An exceptionally long-strider, he found it difficult to reach balls normally within range. There was nothing he could loosen. Not even a zipper in those days.

Thirty-seven minutes later he was blasted out of the tourney, 6-1, 6-2.

Before leaving the court he stood for a long moment peering at the supposed flag of his country, a gesture translated by the crowd as patriotic and perhaps seeking forgiveness for his poor showing.

Actually, he was figuring the easiest way up the pole.

Sitting in his office the next day, speculating on the size of the gate, Perry Jones was disturbed from his reveries by an assistant who burst through the door gesticulating wildly and muttering gibberish. Jones followed him to investigate.

He saw, substituting for the Irish flag, a pair of soiled white flannels, the long legs flapping in the stiff wind.

Here is another one, a tongue in cheek tale, written by my biographer, Cy Rice, that should appeal to every person who ever coveted a cup.

THE KING AND MR. BELL

To the French Riviera, that crescented, craggy coastline of Southern France where rugged mountains wet their rocky feet in a warm blue sea, there came a turbanned visitor from India, the Rajah of a small but prosperous province. Accompanying the Rajah was a retinue of servants carrying the luggage and accouterments associated with gentlemen of wealth. With them was a man lugging an oblong case. The case contained six tennis rackets. He was known simply as Mr. Bell.

Mr. Bell was a somewhat mysterious character along the fashionable Riviera in the early 1930's who might be described in Indian social circles as being "from the wrong side of the jungle." An avid tennis devotee and player of fair ability himself, the Rajah had, for the convenience of a partner always within beck and call, hired Mr. Bell as a secretary.

While Mr. Bell might fall flat on his punctuation trying to insert a semi-colon in its proper place during letter dictation, he rarely missed an overhead smash at the net. His forehand

carried the sting of a cobra. He hit his slightly undercut backhand on the rise; and when forced into a defensive lob, he
employed a short upward stroke which generated so much
top spin that when the ball landed it jumped toward the fenc-
ings, making it almost irretrievable.

Taciturn, phlegmatic Mr. Bell had one weakness. It was
not a fleshly one, nor the pop of champagne corks or the click
of roulette chips. His basic impotency was tennis trophies. In
plain language, Mr. Bell was cup-happy. On days of tournament finals when trophies were placed alongside the court
on a table, Mr. Bell might be observed standing before the
glittering array, his body slightly bowed in an almost reverent
position, while softly murmuring admiring words.

This overpowering passion for cups often drained the
pockets of his tennis flannels of every rupee put into them
by the Rajah. Each tournament he entered found Mr. Bell
long and earnestly studying the entry list in all six events in
which he was scheduled to play—the singles, doubles, mixed
doubles, and the three handicaps for the same events. If
placed in what appeared to be a favorable position of the
draw, and his chances of winning seemed bright, Mr. Bell
approached the tournament director with a stunning proposition.

"Sahib," he would say, "the cup in the men's singles is very
small."

Before the startled director could frame a reply, Mr. Bell
interjected, "I will personally replace it with a larger one if
you have no objections." This he invariably did. There never
were any objections.

King Gustav of Sweden, royalty's most enthusiastic tennis
player, was on the Riviera that season. While the King pos-
sessed a forehand, the elbow of which rose like a broom handle wielded by an energetic housewife, he had never,
throughout his tennis-playing career, tasted defeat, an ac-

complishment due solely to the courtesy of opponents. The King played a fair game, comparable to a Sunday-only business man on a public court. Perhaps in a town such as Toledo, Ohio, he might have ranked ninth in the veterans' class; surely first in the septuagenarian, if such a division existed. Tennis decorum called for the King to win—but make it close. It was a must. An infraction meant social oblivion. There were no transgressors.

The kindly King took a fancy to the Rajah, inviting him, together with Baron Gottfried Von Cram, the great German Internationalist, and other net luminaries to be his guests and play at the Stockholm summer palace courts. Mr. Bell was included.

The invitation was readily accepted. After a series of gay social activities centering around the palace, the players grouped one evening, without the presence of Mr. Bell, and decided that to repay the King for his graciousness they would stage a select tennis tournament. Naturally the King would be the victor. Near the conclusion of the meeting there was a long moment of silence. All eyes were on the Rajah. He sensed the reason.

Arising, he said, reassuringly, "Do not worry, gentlemen. I will talk to Mr. Bell."

Karl Schroeder, Swedish champion, flexed his muscles and suggested, "Are you sure you wouldn't like me to handle the situation?"

The Rajah, understanding the implication, smiled. "I see what you mean. No thanks, just leave him to me."

That evening the Rajah unwound his yards of turban, sat comfortably in a chair and dispatched a servant for Mr. Bell. The secretary arrived, bowed respectfully and asked, "Dictation?"

"Yes," said the Rajah. "Dictation. Very important dictation."

Mr. Bell whipped out his notebook, unscrewed the cap of his fountain pen. "I am ready, Master," he announced.

The Rajah said crisply, "My dictation is verbal. Pay close attention. We are playing in a tennis tournament here at the palace. The King is competing. The King must win! Do you understand?"

"Yes, Master. The King must win."

"Then it is fully understood?"

"Yes, Master. Is that all, Master?"

"Not quite." The Rajah pointed his long dark forefinger at Mr. Bell. "Remember this. If you meet the King and he does not win, you lose your job."

Mr. Bell nodded. "Anything else, Master?"

"Yes," the Rajah said grimly. "There is something else. If you disobey my orders you will lose not only your job, but upon return to my province you will also lose your head."

"Have no fear, Master," said Mr. Bell.

"I have none," said the Rajah. "The fear will all be on your part."

Next day the draw was made. The King and Mr. Bell were in opposite halves. As the competition was formidable it was considered a certainty that Mr. Bell would fall by the wayside in the early rounds. However, Mr. Bell confounded the prophets by playing the best tennis of his life. The coolness of the Swedish climate seemed to inoculate him with super-human energy. He scampered around the court like an electrically-charged rabbit. At week's end he was in the finals, pitted against King Gustav, the world's only undefeated player.

The day of the finals was dark and drizzly. Toward midday a fine mist developed which gradually slacked and died by afternoon. A tarpaulin was unrolled from the court and the contestants began warming up. The white balls were fuzzy, ivory spheroids against the backdrop of bleakness.

"Don't worry, gentlemen," the Rajah whispered to his friends, "Mr. Bell understands."

And it seemed that Mr. Bell did. Under the overcast sky the King took the first set handily, 6-1, and jumped into a 2-0 lead in the second. It was a two out of three set match. Everything was going according to plans. Those in on the plan breathed easily.

When it became obvious that increasing winds had chased the rain away, it was decided to move the cup—a huge one subscribed to by the players—to its official resting place on a table by the umpire's stand. This was done. It was hardly noticeable, obscured by the blackness in the Heavens.

With his own service coming up, the King swung into a comfortable 4-0 lead. Just then the sun burst from its cloudy imprisonment. Bright light flooded the court at precisely the exact moment the King hit a weak return that barely cleared the net close to the alley near the umpire's stand. Mr. Bell, anticipating the shot, came charging in, brought back his racket and to the amazement of the spectators barely touched the ball. It dribbled to his feet and looked more like a ping pong stroke than tennis. Something had diverted his attention.

The cup!

The full glory of the sun shone on the resplendent trophy. Silvery light rays reflected off its metal surface. It was a dazzling sight. Mr. Bell stood transfixed. Seemingly with a great effort he tore his eyes from the trophy, trotting back for service return.

From this moment on the entire complexion of the match changed. Mr. Bell mercilessly hammered the ball to all corners of the court. He was the composite of a Tilden, a Budge, a Kramer.

Mr. Bell took twelve games in a row, gave the dazed King a cursory handshake over the net, rushed to the cup, clasped it

lovingly into his arms and ran from the court in panic haste.
He has never been seen or heard from since.

The concluding story comes from the files of Sam Balter,
Southern California sportscaster and columnist. It's an oldie
from his *One For The Book* collection. Sam relates it with
warmth and compassion, and to borrow a phrase from TV, it
has more strength in audio than in video.

A NEED FOR EACH OTHER

Tragedy is a grim, unwelcome ghost that stalks the lives of
humans, raising its unseen hand to strike when least expected. It hits hard and fast and has the power to blot out or
alter the course of a life. Tragedy is ubiquitous and visits unexpected places like a tennis court during the French Championships under the radiant serenity of a Paris sky.

France was a tennis-minded nation long before its Four
Musketeers—Cochet, LaCoste, Borotra, and Brugnon—began three years of invincibility. In those pre-Musketeer days
the name of Andre Gobert cropped up with frequency. He
was a stylist, a crafty change of pace wizard whose game was
fortified by a smashing first service.

His service was never more devastating than the afternoon
he was playing the flashy but unsteady William Laurentz in
the finals of the French Championships. Early in the match
Gobert's cannonball thundered off the wood of Laurentz'
racket, caroming into his right eye. Laurentz threw his hands
to his eye, lurched blindly around, staggered against the backstop and slumped unconscious to the court.

Gobert vaulted the net, rushing to aid the stricken player.
There was little he could do. A few hours later a surgeon removed Laurentz' eye. Gobert paced the floor of the hospital
waiting room, nervously clasping and unclasping his hands.

The tragedy weighed heavily upon him, and although in the strictest sense the blame was not his, he nevertheless felt a strong responsibility.

After a recuperation period, Laurentz was back on the court, once more engaged in the tennis wars. But it was a different Laurentz. No longer was he the impetuous, daring player whose game rose to brilliant, dizzy heights and then often slumped to netting easy returns. Caution was the keynote of his play, a one-eyed conservative, far removed from his former formidable self.

Gobert and Laurentz had contrasting personalities stemming from their backgrounds. Gobert came from a modest family; Laurentz was a rich and dashing figure. Neither one had ever sought out the other as a doubles partner. Now Gobert practically implored Laurentz to form a tandem. He consented.

They immediately became a feared combination, losing few matches. Gobert seemed to have an uncanny knack of sensing Laurentz' blind spots. Standing near the center service line he covered many shots difficult for Laurentz to reach. Such tactics improved Gobert's footwork and provided him with a keen anticipatory sense.

Actually he was trying to atone for that awful moment in the French Championships, by playing the role of benefactor and big brother. He became irrevocably bound to the man whose singles game he had ruined for all time, and he felt he was paying him back by becoming his partner in the world's best tennis duo.

Neither man ever spoke of the incident. Laurentz, it appeared, had shut the door of his mind on it and never cared to open it, even a tiny bit. His attitude bothered Gobert. Gobert wished to talk it out. Better, he thought, if Laurentz would be openly resentful and speak the words that were in his heart. He began to almost take offense at what he considered was mock bravery in his partner's attitude, a too martyr-like approach.

If Gobert believed that Laurentz harbored any pent-up intolerance that would some day burst the leashes of self-control, he was wrong. Laurentz kept his mouth shut, and some surmised that he thought Gobert unnecessarily charitable.

Despite what may have been smoldering under the surface, they played beautifully together, although tension mounted with each tournament. They became high strung. Gobert was too patronizing, overly solicitous. It was inevitable that the pair should break up. There were no arguments, no discussion, just a wordless parting due to each knowing the other's instincts.

Both entered the singles at Wimbledon, England. Even though Gobert had played no singles since the accident, he was a far superior player than at any time of his life. He was an odds-on-favorite to capture the title, a title tantamount to world supremacy. A large delegation of Frenchmen crossed the channel to support him.

With Gobert watching from the stand, Laurentz fell victim to a greatly inferior player in the first round. Following his ex-partner to the court, Gobert barely eked out a bitter five-set match with an opponent he should have romped through. Tennis writers could not fathom his poor showing.

Only Gobert and Laurentz knew what was wrong. Still blaming himself for the old tragedy, Gobert could not distort the clear-cut image of the flight of the ball striking Laurentz in the eye. It was similar to the hackneyed movie plot of the pugilist, who after accidentally killing an opponent in the ring, can never fight again. As his own shot once effaced the sight of Laurentz, so did the memory of it now hinder his every move.

It was a miracle that he reached the finals, being on the

verge of defeat in nearly every match, only his splendid physical conditioning proving the determining factor. His game during the finals was at the lowest ebb ever witnessed by Wimbledon spectators, and the former great singles player was easily crushed.

Moved by what he saw, the heart of Laurentz melted into compassion. It became clear to both of them that individually they were worthless, but together, bound securely by the tragedy, they could be unbeatable.

When Gobert, filed from the court after his loss, Laurentz caught up with him, touched his arm and murmured, "Too bad, Andre."

Gobert smiled and asked, "Will we play together again?"

"But of course," Laurentz said.

A real friendship existed at last.

Index